The Mystery Fancier

Volume 8, Number 4
July/August 1986

TABLE OF CONTENTS

MYSTERIOUSLY SPEAKING	Page 1
That Pawn-Shop Gypsy By Bob Sampson	Page 9
Mickey Spillane's Mike Hammer: The Great Cover-Up By Jeff Banks	Page 17
The Rural Policeman in American Mystery Fiction By George Dove	Page 21
Scandinavian Mystery Scene By K Arne Blom	Page 24
The Cream of Queen By Frank Floyd	Page 27
IT'S ABOUT CRIME By Marvin Lachman	Page 29
REEL MURDERS By Walter Albert	Page 34
VERDICTS Book Reviews	Page 37
THE DOCUMENTS IN THE CASE Letters	Page 48

The Mystery Fancier
(USPS:428-590)
is edited and published bi-monthly by
Guy M. Townsend
1711 Clifty Drive
Madison, IN 47250

SUBSCRIPTION RATES: Second-class mail, U.S. and Canada, $15.00 per year (6 issues); first-class mail, U.S. and Canada, $18.00; overseas surface mail, $15.00; overseas air mail, $21.00. Overseas subscribers please pay in international money order, check drawn on U.S. bank, or currency; no checks drawn on foreign banks, please.

Single copy price: $3.00
Second-class postage paid at Madison, Indiana
Copyright 1986 by Guy M. Townsend
All rights reserved for contributors
ISSN:0146-3160

Cover by Lari Davidson

Thanks for sticking with me. I knew, when I put TMF on hold more than two years ago, that it would return, but, with small publications of this type having such a high death rate, the rest of you could certainly have been forgiven for having your doubts and for asking for a refund of the unused portion of your subscriptions. To my considerable astonishment and even greater delight, only a handful--not more that six or eight--asked for a refund, and most of those were people who had only joined TMF within the last year or so. The rest of you people were wonderfully loyal, and I love you for it.

So here it is, packed with good articles and reviews, but, understandably, a bit shy on letters. I look forward to a return of the lively and lengthy letters section in the next issue, but I'm not entirely sorry that it's a bit slim this time around, since it gives me an excuse for taking up even more than my usual amount of space with what amounts to a letter of my own to you folks, making a start on bringing you up to date on the continuing saga of Guy M. Townsend, Boy Wonder. Given my regrettable verbosity it will only be a start, and I'll have to wait until 8:5 to go into such matters as what it is like to have your first novel (which is only marginally less precious than your first child) trashed mercilessly, and what it is like to have a book you have published for another win an Edgar, and what the future likely holds in store for TMF (such as a laser printer, maybe in time for 9:1). The two matters I discuss at such great length below are not necessarily the most important--they are just the ones I started on first, and when I saw how long they had run on I decided to go with what I had and cover the rest later. I need letters, reviews, and articles, so send them along asap. (I'll be hitting you for money later.)

LAW SCHOOL

Law school was in turns exciting, stimulating, terrifying, humiliating, unbelievably time-consuming, and down-right incredibly hard work. Having performed respectably in graduate school while acquiring my M.A. and my Ph.D., I anticipated being able to breeze through law school without working up a sweat. In fact, however, my anticipations remained unfulfilled from beginning to end. The first thing I discovered was that the skills, whatever they may be, which make a good graduate student are not the same skills that make a good law student. Not only is the subject matter of law school completely different, but law schools in America employ the diabolical Socratic method for teaching courses, which, like sex, has got to be experienced to be believed. And what is even worse, law school requires an entirely different way of thinking than does graduate school, and trying to cast off the habits of a lifetime of study while trying to acquire a new mind set practically overnight was one of the hardest things I have ever tried to do, and my grades, while respectable, were nothing compared to my graduate school grades.

That's a bit deceptive, though. To graduate from graduate school (at least from any graduate school I've ever heard of or had dealings with) one has to finish ones course of study with a grade point of at least 3.0 on a 4.0 scale. This is a B average. It could be argued--and is argued by some defenders of the present system--that graduate students simply perform at a higher level than undergraduates, or, to put it another way, that while C students are common in undergraduate school, B students are common in graduate school. Then again, it could be argued that grades are inflated in graduate school, and that the same performance that would earn a C in an undergraduate course will earn a B in a graduate course. In law school, one only has to have a 2.0 grade point to graduate (again, on a 4.0 scale), and the easy though entirely mistaken conclusion that can be drawn from this is that it is easier to get a law degree than it is to get a graduate degree. In fact, though, a C grade, which is almost entirely unheard of in graduate school, is commonplace in law school, and I have seen excellent students almost cry with relief upon receiving a C. Even an occasional D is no disgrace, and Fs are not unheard of--I know several good (though not outstanding) law students who have failed courses and had to take them over before they could graduate.

Another diabolical aspect of law school is its testing system. The grade in a course is based entirely on the student's performance on a single test (usually three hours long) given at the end of the semester. Have an argument with the spouse the night before and take the final in a bad frame of mind, and you run a good chance of blowing an entire semester. It's an outrageous system, but that's the way it's done. This is particularly hard on an old geezer like myself who has for years been systematically killing off brain cells with daily doses of gin and tonic and whose memory is about as long as a bankrupt's line of credit. When a professor spends more than four months covering the law of corporations, for example, and then expects me to perform well on an exam covering everything from day one onward, he is bound to be disappointed with my performance (which he was).

The evening law program in which I was enrolled takes four years to complete. That breaks down to eight regular semesters plus at least one semester of summer school. Owing to my advanced age, I foolishly petitioned for permission to graduate a year early, and some sadists in the administration approved my request. Now, in order to graduate early I had to take a full load in summer school for three years running, plus I had to take sixteen hours of courses in each of my last two regular semesters (and twelve to fourteen hours is a full load for a **full-time day student**). So I had six regular semesters and three summer semesters. The regular semesters last between four and five months, and the summer semesters last for seven to eight weeks. In the six regular semesters, in which I was tested on material that I had covered four to five months earlier, I never once came out with as much as a 3.0 grade point, but in the three summer semesters, where the final was no more than two months after the first day of class, I never once came out with less than a 3.0 grade point. Since I didn't study any harder in the summer than in the fall or the spring, I attribute the difference to my failing memory.

I entered law school expecting to finish in the top ten percent, but when the first semester grades came out I was chagrined to find that I was barely in the top twenty-five percent—and that was the good news, folks. Nearly ninety people were enrolled in the evening division when the first semester started, but there were only sixty-seven of us left when finals came around. I was in the top quarter of that sixty-seven (but only just). Unfortunately, the attrition didn't stop there. Every semester our class consisted of fewer and fewer students, and at the end of my third year (my classmates still had a year to go) fewer than forty of our original number remained. It will come as no surprise to you, although I confess that it did to me, that simply holding ones on in a situation like this means that ones class standing **relative to the survivors** declines steadily as the class size diminishes. I mean, none of the people who ranked higher me were flunking out or quitting, and every person below me who departed left me that much closer to the bottom. The result was that by the time I finished law school my grade point was about the same as it had been that first semester and I was about the same distance from the top of the class, but, instead of being in the top quarter, I was damned lucky to even be in the top half. And that, folks, is down right embarrassing to someone who has over the years come to think of himself as a Smart Person.

And that about covers my adventures in law school. I managed to win a few book awards and was a member of the law review, so I didn't disgrace myself—well, at least not too badly—but it certainly was a humbling experience. The lawyers among you (and there are more than a few) will understand and perhaps even sympathize with what I've said above. The rest of you who have not undergone the ordeal will just have to take my word for it. I definitely would not recommend it as a pleasant way to spend the first third of ones fifth decade. What's more, I wore out two new cars in three years driving 600 miles a week, and I lost most of the remaining hairs that sparsely dotted my balding pate (a few, frizzy, gray strands remain to keep me, just barely, out of the Kojak class).

MYSTERY AND DETECTIVE MONTHLY

One of the nice things that happened while I was busy elsewhere was the creation, by Bob Napier, of a mystery "letterzine" called **Mystery & Detective Monthly**. As the term letterzine implies, the publication consists almost entirely of letters (imagine TMF's "The Documents in the Case" expanded to fill most of a magazine) with a listing of recent mystery releases and a few reviews by Jeff Smith thrown in for good measure. For the first fifteen issues I could find nothing to quarrel about or object to in MDM, but in his editorial column in number sixteen (November 1985) Bob wrote as follows:

> Now on to something not so pleasant. Back when John Nieminski did his "interview" with S.A. Roscoe mention was made that a certain detective story writer, whose titles include **The Big Enchilada** and **Sleaze**, was a draft dodger. I've finally confirmed that this is a fact. Therefore I won't have that person's name in my magazine. This does not apply to "New Releases"

Mysteriously   4   Speaking ...

because Jeff's the boss there and I don't tell him what
to do. But I'm the honcho of the letters and I refuse to
transcribe any further reference to this person or his
work.

I'll try to explain briefly. It's not because I loved
the Viet Nam war or hated dissidents--I was involved in
each at various times. But when a man's number comes
up he's got to go because if he doesn't, if he runs away,
then another man has to go in his place. And I won't
abide anyone who'd make another take his place on the
line. It's that simple.

I'm removing this person's books from my home
and for all I care the son of a bitch can squat in
Canada until the glaciers melt.

Now if you were a subscriber to MDM at the time you may have
noticed that the subject was never again brought up in MDM and you
may have concluded from that silence that no one found Bob's action
worthy of comment. If you did conclude that, you would have been
wrong. I have learned from several quarters that there were a
number people who were offended by Bob's action and who expressed
their unhappiness either to him or to others, even going so far as to
sever their connections with the magazine. Of course I didn't know
all this at the beginning. All I knew was that a friend of mine had
taken what I thought to be a very unwise position and, despite the
fact that fall semester finals were looming large, I took an afternoon
off to think about and then write a letter to Bob Napier as editor of
MDM. My letter never appeared in MDM, nor did any other response
to what Bob had done, and Bob's response to my letter was marked
"not for publication." I will, of course, honor Bob's request and not
quote from his letter, but I think that what I said in my letter to
MDM needs to be aired, so here it is, in full:

You are wrong, Bob--one-hundred percent dead
wrong. And if I can't convince you of that fact, then I
face the truly sorrowful necessity of having to ask you
to terminate my subscription to MDM and refund
whatever balance I have coming. I honestly don't want
the money back, but neither do I want to support, in
even the smallest way, a publication which condemns
individuals out of hand for holding views of which the
publication's editor disapproves. I refer, of course, to
your pronouncement in MDM 16 regarding L.A.
Morse--which was far, far beneath you, my friend.

I am absolutely, morally certain that there were
many people who dodged the draft out of sheer
cowardice and others who ran away out of a selfish
unwillingness to do their duty as citizens. I am just as
certain that many of our soldiers in Vietnam were guilty
of rape and murder and other acts of brutality and
astonishing inhumanity. I have as little use for one
group as for the other.

On the other hand, I am no less certain that
many of our soldiers went to Vietnam because they
wanted to do their duty to their country and wanted to
help secure the benefits of freedom for the people of
that little country. And I also know with equal
certainty that there were people who believed with all
their hearts and consciousness that what we were doing

in Vietnam was wrong, and who, rather than put themselves in a position of having to kill for what they believed was an immoral cause, exiled themselves from their families and their friends and their country. I have as much respect for one as for the other.

No sane individual will deny that there were selfish, unprincipled cowards among the draft resisters, any more than any sane individual will deny that some of our soldiers did participate in massacres, did rape Vietnamese women, did murder helpless civilians, even children, even infants. But not all draft resisters were selfish, unprincipled cowards, any more than all soldiers were murderers and rapists.

It would be outrageous for an editor to say that he intended to ban from his publication any mention of any writer who had participated in the Vietnam War. What you propose to do is not one bit less outrageous—nor one whit less reprehensible.

You say "when a man's number comes up he's got to go because if he doesn't, if he runs away, then another man has to go in his place. And I won't abide anyone who'd make another take his place on the line." That statement, besides being suspect for being of the "good German" variety, suffers the fatal defect of being specious. It assumes that there are no circumstances under which refusal to serve one's country can be justified (an assumption which this country rejected pretty comprehensively at Nuernburg) and that the next fellow on the list is incapable of making decisions on his own. By refusing to fight, the draft resister didn't make another take his place on the line; he just put the next man on the list in the same position he had been in—the position of having to make a difficult moral decision.

Lest you or any of MDM's readers think that I'm making these arguments to justify any actions of my own, let me point out that I had completed my military service before the Vietnam conflict hotted up (I was on active duty from 1961 to 1963) and was never in the least danger of having to choose between putting myself in a position of having to kill for a cause that I believed was unjust or sticking to my principles and leaving behind, perhaps for ever, my family and my friends and my very life. I like to think that I would have had the courage to leave the country rather than submit to the draft, but I'll never know.

Another thing. You seem to be operating under the delusion, common to us magazine editors, that MDM is yours: "I am the honcho of the letters and I refuse to transcribe any further reference to this person or his work." (Why on earth not? Transcribing references to Joseph Hansen hasn't make you a homosexual, has it? And I doubt very much that any of MDM's readers have interpreted the fact that you have transcribed references to Hansen as being endorsement on your part of homosexuality.) You are confusing the concept of power with the concept of right. If I arm myself with a loaded pistol and I successfully break into your home and surprise you helpless and unarmed in your bed, I certainly have the power to take your life, but no one would argue that I have the right. As editor, you unquestionably have the power to expunge from all letters any reference to any author who holds views of which you disapprove, but do you have the right? I think not. What's more, I believe that MDM's readers also think not. If I'm mistaken about this, then I don't belong among their number.

Censorship is abhorrent, especially in a publication of this sort. You have frequently said or intimated that MDM belongs to its contributors, but if you persist in this action you will be belying that claim and making it clear to everyone that MDM belongs only to you and to those who are willing to accept you as their censor.

Bob replied a couple of weeks later, in a letter marked "not for publication." I will honor that request in so far as not quoting from it, but I will say that in it he utterly rejected my plea, accused me of employing censorship in TMF, and refused to refund the balance of my subscription to MDM. I responded to his letter with a long one of my own (I was between semesters and was able to find the hours that the letter required). In that letter I replied in detail to points he raised in his letter, frequently quoting his own words back at him. I cannot, for that reason, transcribe my reply in its entirety, since that would violate his request that I not publish what he had written. What appears below, therefore, is my letter of 2 January 1986, with portions deleted which would violate Bob's do-not-quote request:

> ... Here's a guy about whom you evidently know absolutely nothing except that he is a mystery writer who went to Canada rather than go to Vietnam, and you have so finely developed a moral olfactory sense that you know right off that he is so odious and despicable as to require proscription. Well, Bob, I find rape odious and infant homicide despicable, and both are intensely personal with me. I also know that American soldiers raped women and murdered babies in Vietnam, but my nose is not sensitive enough to enable me to sniff out the odium and despicability given only the notice that someone served in Vietnam. Therefore, I'm willing to give every Vietnam vet that I encounter the benefit of the doubt and treat each of them with the respect that most of them deserve. I do this because I think that the principles of fairness and justice--upon which, incidentally, our nation was built--require it. It's an awful shame that your supernatural sense has overpowered this sense of fairness and justice in you. I wonder what it was that you went to Vietnam to fight for? It obviously wasn't for the old-fashioned American idea that you don't condemn a person until you know the facts....
>
> I suggest that your understanding of the words editor and censor is seriously flawed. Webster's Second defines a censor as "one who acts as an overseer of morals and conduct," while it defines an editor as "one who prepares the work of another for publication; one who revises, corrects, arranges, or annotates, a text, document, or book." There are, of course, other definitions, but I find none which describes an editor as

one who imposes his prejudices on those who write for and read his publication. You have set yourself up as "overseer of [the] morals and conduct" of L.A. Morse, and you have proscriptively censored—not edited—him out of existence, so far as your magazine is concern.

Look, Bob, I'm not saying that you ought to love Morse as a brother. For all I know, he may very well have gone to Canada because he was a coward, or because he didn't love his country, or for any of a number of other despicable reasons. All I'm saying is that you are wrong for condemning him out of hand in this "all niggers is ign'ernt" fashion. If you find out that his reasons for going to Canada were ignoble--and you can't simply say that the mere going to Canada is **ipso facto** ignoble--then you tell me about it and I will join you in condemning him. But the way to deal with the problem is not to proscribe all mention of him--thus running the risk of being compared with such self-righteous, hypocritical, know-nothings as Jerry Falwell, who would suppress every step of progress in the biological and physical sciences (except, of course, for the technology needed to produce polyester) to protect their dogma from the insidious attack of logic and reason--but, rather, to allow discussion. That's what your magazine purports to be--a forum for discussion of matters relating to mysteries and detection. You do your cause a disservice by taking a stance which says, in effect, that you are so blind and intolerant that you are not only willing to condemn people out of hand for their actions and beliefs, but you actively refuse to consider any of the facts of the case, however mitigating or even exculpatory they may be.

Let's look at a situation that happened many times in Vietnam. Maybe it happened to you or to someone you knew over there. An American soldier kills a ten or eleven year old child. Sounds odious and despicable to me, stated like that. Maybe not as odious and despicable as, say, an American war-resister going to Canada to avoid the draft, but still pretty bad. But if we were to consider the facts in the first case we might discover that at the time the solder killed the child, the child was himself doing his damnedest to kill the American. Ain't it wonderful how the stench has disappeared? Now maybe, just maybe, if we were to consider the facts in the second case before we condemned the war-resister, we might find that there is no stench there either. But you evidently can't be troubled with trying to see the other fellow's point of view. "Don't confuse me with facts," the infamous Indiana congressman (R) said during the Watergate crisis, "my mind's made up." (To this state's everlasting credit, the bugger was roundly defeated in the subsequent election.)...

We disagree about a great many things, Bob, but I would have bet that there were at least two things on which we were in complete agreement: that that elusive thing we call truth can only emerge and flourish where there is a free interchange of ideas; and that the only freedom that deserves the name is the freedom to have and express ones own beliefs. What disturbs me so much about your decision is that it indicates that you don't subscribe to either.

About my request that you refund the balance of my subscription should you decline to reconsider your decision. As I said in my earlier letter, I can't in good conscience contribute in even the smallest way to a publication in which censorship is used to support the editor's prejudices, and I was startled by your refusal to refund my money. I've demanded refunds from a number of publications over the years (usually on matters of principle, such as this, but sometimes simply because I didn't think the publication was worth the price, which certainly is not the case with MDM), though never before a publication in our field, and not once have I been refused. In fact, it never entered my mind that you or anyone would even consider refusing, and to my knowledge you are the only publisher of a going publication which has ever done so. Life is just full of surprises. Well, now, since my purpose in requesting a refund of my subscription was to refrain from giving support to your publication, and since telling you to discontinue sending me copies even though you are keeping my money would have just the opposite effect, I am put in the peculiar position—assuming you remain unswayed by my labors—of best being able to withdraw my support by continuing to receive copies of MDM until my balance is exhausted. So be it.

(Just to keep the record straight and to make certain that the reason for this brouhaha is not lost in this excess of verbiage, my request for a refund was made conditional upon your refusal to reconsider your decision to proscribe L.A. Morse from MDM, an action you regard as editorial in nature, while I claim that it constitutes censorship. What I am asking you to do is to allow us subscribers to discuss Morse or any other writer or mystery-related subject in MDM, provided our letters meet your **editorial** requirements, always reserving to yourself, of course, the right to wade in with editorial comments denouncing, excoriating, vilifying, and just plain bad-mouthing the bugger to your reactionary heart's content. If you'll do that, then I'll instantly withdraw my request for a refund and begin to plan for that day in late summer when I'll be able to sit down and write my first letter to MDM. If you won't, then I'll just have to get by without your fine magazine once my current subscription expires.)

I failed to persuade him to reconsider, and my subscription expired with issue #24, which I received just last week. In none of the issues since 16 has any discussion of this matter appeared in the pages of MDM--but not, as I hope is now clear, because people did not feel strongly about what Bob was doing or because they did not write to MDM to express those feelings. There has been no discussion in MDM because Bob has been censoring the letters. Now that I have brought the subject out into the light, I offer TMF as a forum for any such discussion which may have been repressed elsewhere, and I welcome a response from Bob which is for publication.

That Pawn-Shop Gypsy

Robert Sampson

Queen Victoria's reign entered its final decade. Sherlock Holmes practiced in Baker Street and consecutive issues of **The Strand**. And through magazine and dime novels rose a tide of detectives, each curious, unique, unusual.

To be a detective no professional qualification was required—only an inappropriate occupation. So literature was refreshed by the activities of detecting bootblacks, Irishmen, farmers, sailors, lip readers, Indians, costermongers, and women. Unlikely detectives all.

Most of these amateur investigators performed their intuitive miracles only briefly. A story or two, then they melted away, uncelebrated, unremembered, as transient as a spring breeze.

Others, equally transient, somehow got themselves into books; and, because books, even bad books, endure after magazines are forgotten, a few archaic detectives survive to the present, startling artifacts of our former simplicity.

Which is to explain why we stand here in a bitter November evening, watching a young woman enter a London pawn shop.

> ... a young girl of twenty years stepped into the shop. She was dressed in a dark red garment made of some coarse stuff and over this she wore a short black coat. Her hands were bare, and also her head, save for a scarlet handkerchief, which was carelessly twisted round her magnificent black hair. The face was of the true Romney type: Oriental in its contour and hue, with arched eye-brows over large dark eyes, and a thin-lipped mouth beautifully shaped, under a delicately-curved nose. Face and figure were those of a woman who needed palms and desert sands and golden sunshine, hot and sultry, for an appropriate background; yet this Eastern beauty appeared out of the fog like some dead Syrian princess and presented herself in all her rich loveliness to the astounded eyes of the old pawn-broker.
> (Fergus Hume, **Hagar of the Pawn-Shop, The Gypsy Detective**. London: Greenhill Books, 1985, p. 9.)

The young woman is Hagar Stanley, a full-blooded gypsy. Her adventures are contained in the book, **Hagar of the Pawn-Shop, The Gypsy Detective**, published in 1897 and written by that industrious scribbler, Fergus Hume (1859-1932).

Hume had tough luck all his life. He published nearly 150 books, made a fortune for others, but lived all his life on the crumbling edge of poverty. He poured out unsaleable plays, only one of them ever accepted—that by Sir Henry Irving, who promptly died; the play was never produced.

It was Hume's luck, the consequence of his former life, he thought, spent as a French nobleman. He remembered that clearly, particularly recalling how he was guillotined, releasing his soul to a dubious afterlife as a hack writer.

Hume was born in England. While he was still a child, his family moved to New Zealand. There he was educated and entered the law. Moving to Melbourne, he worked as a law-office clerk while writing unwanted plays. Money problems ground him. He researched the fiction market, discovered that the mystery novels of Gaboriau sold well. He composed a mystery novel, **The Mystery of a Hansom Cab**, selling the copyright for fifty pounds. It was the error of his life. The book, published in London in 1887, sold 340,000 copies within a year. Hume got nothing but the fifty pounds, and a good deal of unspendable fame.

Thereafter he moved to England to write plays no one wanted and fiction which was never as successful as **The Hansom Cab**. He died regretting his excesses as a French nobleman. Lifelong bad luck.

The Mystery of a Hansom Cab has kept Hume's name alive. Those who have read the book say that it is tediously long-winded, where it is readable at all. You cannot say that about **Hagar of the Pawn-Shop**. That book is certainly readable, particularly if you cultivate a relaxed attitude toward sentiment and coincidence.

As for detection, Hagar rarely detects. Literary detection lines up observed facts and reasons to an orderly conclusion. That is not Hagar's way. She is, first of all, a young lady of hard common sense who happens to run a pawn shop. Her mind is uneducated but cold, firm, practical—above all else, practical. She is a puzzle solver. She enjoys ciphers. But ratiocination is not her thing.

As a detective, she rarely cuts deeply enough. True, she solves two murders, recovers a pair of treasures by untangling ciphers, and foils a blackmailer. She also learns the inner history of a failed engagement. But all this is small change. You would expect even an early feminine detective to accomplish more. However, there are reasons why she does not.

To begin with, Hume was writing before 1900, using fiction conventions from even earlier times. He was not writing detective stories but adventure stories faintly tinged by mystery. He lacked our advantage of eighty-five years of familiarity with the mystery form.

The development of the mystery is so obvious to us today that we wonder impatiently at the dullness of the early writers. How could they fail to see the rainbow road gleaming ahead of them into the future?

But patience, patience. We are very wise now. And writers, poor stumbling things, write for the moment. Often they even ignore the critical standards of the future. It is a sad fault.

Other matters cause Hagar to be a less-than-technically-proficient detective. She appeared in only a single series. That began with an Introduction to get her into the pawn shop and present a few of the continuing characters, and it closed with a chapter taking her out of the shop and concluding the series by disposing of the characters as a housewife disposes of crumbs. Between front and back were ten stories, each built around an item pawned at the shop. It was at once the gimmick and the chief technical stumbling block.

Some mystery clings to that pawned object. Hagar's curiosity flares. Now and then she leaves the shop to investigate further.

More frequently, she is unable to leave—for she is a working woman, after all. She sniffs mystery but cannot chase it. So it is up to the kindly author to whisk away the reader and show what happened later.

As a result, some stories contain major shifts of viewpoint. They angle off to violent adventures, and, while interesting adventures, they get very far from the pawn shop. By sheer inadvertence, they reduce Hagar to a walk-on character in her own series.

The ten adventures, framed between the first and final chapters, are weakly chronological. The pawn-shop scene and a few sustaining characters link them together. The end result is one of those loose books, like Edgar Wallace's **Four-Square Jane** or Anna Katherine Green's **The Golden Slipper**—not quite an episodic novel, not quite a short-story collection, but a limber combination of the forms.

The opening chapter, "The Coming of Hagar," gives enough background information, character relationships, and situation to sink a barge. At the risk of drifting you away to Slumberland, the main threads are:

--Crusty old Jacob Dix, stereotype pawnbroker (he is not, however, Jewish), married a gypsy girl in his youth and had a worthless son, Jimmy. Mrs. Dix is long deceased.

--Jimmy has gone Lord knows where and has not reappeared.

--Dix's crony is Vark, a thieves' lawyer and twisting crook himself. He is Dix's executor and his fingers itch for the pawnbroker's wealth.

--Hagar Stanley, that glowing girl, is the niece of Dix's wife. She has fled from her gypsy tribe in the New Forest because a hulking half-breed, Goliath, kept pestering her to get married. The sight of Goliath turns her stomach. When the gypsy king decreed that she marry the hulk, Hagar bolted to London and her closest relative, Dix. She offers to become Dix's servant in exchange for room and board.

--Vark promptly falls in love with Hagar, although she regards him as a cut below Goliath.

--Vark schemes to get Dix to disinherit his son, assuming that he will leave shop and fortune to Hagar, after which Vark plans to marry Hagar and clean up.

--Vark forges a note from Jimmy outlining a plan to kill Dix. Although this is one of the least credible notes in the history of mystery fiction, Dix believes it. He has a stroke and dies, leaving Hagar the executor of his will. --Hagar takes over the pawn shop, intending to run it until Jimmy returns and then turn the business over to him. When Vark proposes to loot the estate with her help, she scorns his nefarious proposal. Gives him the harsh edge of her tongue, she does, and drives him out--after he reveals that Jimmy and Goliath are the same person.

Got all that? Okay, that brings us to Chapter II, "The First Customer and the Florentine Dante," the initial adventure.

"The Florentine Dante" adds some more plot and gives Hagar her first opportunity to solve a puzzle. Into the shop comes a tall, slim, intellectual fellow named Eustace Lorn. He is broke and friendless, poor fellow, and has s personality like a dish of mush and milk. He is, you see, destined to become Hagar's husband and by convention must be ineffectual, inept, and slow in the head. No strong woman ever got a strong man in these stories. If the woman had character and ability, she invariably drew a dish of mush and milk.

Lorn is so hard up he must pawn his chief possession, a Florentine Dante reputed to contain the secret of a family treasure. Lorn, of course, has given up searching the book for the secret. He would.

A week after he pawns the Dante, an elderly man comes to

redeem the book. His name is Treadle, an acquaintance of Lorn's and a grocer. As you may know, grocers are a scheming lot, their eyes slitted and dark. Mystery mantles them. In this they resemble librarians and drug store clerks. Hagar refuses to let Treadle have the book and he skulks muttering away.

Hagar tells Lorn of this incident. Disturbed, he reveals the romantic tale of the Dante—how his miserly Uncle Ben made a fortune in the West Indies and returned to London to clutch every penny. On his death, the fortune could not be found. His will stated that the wealth, carefully hidden, would go to the person locating it. Clues were concealed in the Dante, which Lorn inherited.

Hagar promptly thinks of invisible writing. Soon enough she has located an underlined passage and a tangle of numbers. While Lorn gapes, she deciphers the material. Off they rush to Uncle Ben's former home, there to find Treadle digging frantically around the grounds.

Brushing aside the sinister grocer, Hagar and Lorn locate the buried treasure box. Which contains only a note from Uncle Ben saying that he had no fortune and had lived for years on his relatives' expectations.

A disappointment. Although Lorn received a valuable edition of Dante, slightly marred by a secret notation in lemon juice. In appreciation for Hagar's assistance, he pledges himself to search out Jimmy/Goliath for her. We will hear no more from Lorn until the final chapter, when all loose narrative threads are tied together.

It would be no great favor to you to detail the subsequent stories. they are pleasantly obsolete. Reading them gives you the sensation of trying on grandfather's coat. The tone is leisurely. The language is mildly pedantic and sprinkled with obsolete words, as a window pane is sprinkled by a light shower. Nothing is dramatized that cannot be told in narrative form. And the sentences droop under a relentless burden of cliches--that is what we call them now, not what they called them then.

Hagar, herself, is adored and admired and fussed over. We are told of her beauty, her excellences, her brisk mind and equally brisk tongue. She has the self-confidence of a politician who has been exonerated. For a young barefoot girl who was wandering around the woods just a year ago, she has learned enormous amounts of information--how to evaluate antiques, keep books, read police reports, haggle with customers over a penny.

Also how to live in a groaning slum, she whose life was a constant flow of trees and sky.

Nothing is wrong with her intelligence or her nerve. She will cock a pistol in the face of a hardcase threatening trouble. Or, with just as much urbanity, penetrate Vark's thievish plots at a glance. She is quite the independent young lady, rather brash, perhaps aggressive, undoubtedly she smells of garlic. Undoubtedly she doesn't care.

Although Hume admires her, he simply can't forget that she is a woman and, therefore, not quite the equal of men. This is a tricky attitude to hold, since Hagar is clearly superior to every man appearing in the series--and a fine lot of wimps, dullards, and louts they are.

At intervals, Hume seems to realize that he is giving his lead woman the advantage. Then he rushes to scribble down some appalling generalization about woman: "Now if there be one vice above another which ruins the female sex, it is that of curiosity." That refreshes his mind and allows him to continue his tale about a superior woman without his male conscience aching.

The other characters are so much dough, names tagged by a handful of adjectives. They smirk and posture and plot. Their emotions, if any, are simplified and melodramatic. If unexpected doom finds them out--particularly if they have been messing around with Orientals--their passing raises not a whisper of regret. They are characters in a story. They come and go. Does it make any difference?

The scene is as ill-defined as the characters. The pawn shop is sketched in, a narrow dark place jammed with the debris of lives. Outside the door, the world is barely suggested. The shop sits in Carby's Crescent, Lambeth, poor district, tough district, dangerous district. Other writers have described it for us, as Hume has not.

Out there, rats dance in trash-strewn alleys where the air chokes and the light is the color of mud. Families sprawl on doorsteps and shout from the windows of encrusted rooms, and thud up staircases foul with the failure of hope. Children squirm yelling through the indifferent traffic. Men maneuver for inconsequential advantage. Poverty, ignorance, hope, violence, crime jostle in the street. It is not quite Hell but not far from it.

Even in this sordid place, curious incidents occur that shine like flowers, bright among the squalor. Into the pawn shop steps a customer to place on the counter an object for Hagar's appraisal.

The chances are excellent that the object contains a secret. This jade idol contains directions to a treasure. That elaborate silver crucifix hides a dagger smudged with the blood of a faithless wife. The silver teapot and the Renaissance casket conceal letters that would rend lives if disclosed.' This bobbing, grinning toy in the shape of a Chinese mandarin is stuffed with stolen diamonds, could you only trip the secret catch to see.

Each object generates action. A story results. In many cases, Hagar's role is comparatively minor. She sets matters moving, rather like a woman who slaps the sea and, to her amazement, sees the ripples mound to a tidal wave that sweeps colossal past the horizon.

As in "The Persian Ring" (Chapter XII). No sooner has Hagar touched the ring than up swirls a complexity of double dealing and intrigue. The story rockets clean away from Hagar and the pawn shop. Soon it rockets out of London, ending in Persia. There the ring traps a thief, rather than a traitor, as planned. Of these matters, Hagar learns nothing. The tidal wave has moved completely out of her sight. It is an unsatisfactory position for a heroine filled with the curiosity of her sex.

In "The Copper Key" (Chapter VI), Hagar solves a cipher inscribed along the barrel of a key. Having performed that service, she steps back and the story rushes past her and away. Eventually, her discovery leads to the recovery of a valuable painting and the reconciliation of a father with the girl his son wishes to marry. Hagar isn't there, doesn't know, and apparently never finds out.

She has much more to do in "The Silver Teapot" (Chapter VII). The story is an unashamed tear-jerker. It tells of a blind woman, poor and sick, who has been secretly wronged by another woman. At last the blind woman learns of the other's treachery and forgives her and dies in uncomplaining nobility, faintly augmented by celestial violins and harps. All this tear-blurred emotion because Hagar discovered some letters soldered into the tea pot and read them.

During the events of "The Casket" (Chapter X), Hagar finds other concealed, and indiscreet, letters. She makes short work of a blackmailing valet, then returns the letters to a certain distinguished lady. It is a nice gesture, only slightly spoiled by Hagar's error in giving the letters to the wrong distinguished lady. But even Holmes had his' failures.

In at least two adventures, Hagar performs in the tradition of the amateur detective: she notes vital clues, follows them vigorously, aids Scotland Yard in getting things right, and saves the innocent from the hangman. Both cases are murder mysteries.

In "The Amber Beads" (Chapter III), a black servant is accused of murdering her mistress and pawning her amber necklace. But Hagar's quick eye has caught the significant detail. With the help of Detective Luke Horval of New Scotland Yard, the true criminal is tracked down, and the real murderer confesses in one of those bulky Victorian letters which explains everything and ducks the need to dramatize the ending.

At the conclusion of the case, Detective Horval explodes with admiration for Hagar:

> **Horval:** "You ought to be a man, with that head of yours. You're too good to be a woman."
> **Hagar:** "And not bad enough to be a man."

During the episode of "The Pair of Boots" (Chapter IX), Hagar learns that a pair of pawned boots are the missing evidence in a murder case. She advises Scotland Yard detective Julf, another inadequate man, who gladly consults with her and takes her advice and behaves in a way that would make a modern policeman stagger and rub his eyes.

When Hagar wishes to visit the murder scene, Julf obliges her. He "always believed that two heads were better than one, especially when the second head was that of a woman. He had a great respect for the instinct of the weaker sex."

Instinct or common sense, it's no wonder he trusts Hagar. Once on the scene, she promptly discovers the missing pistol. From that point, all the lies unravel. When Julf discovers a vital piece of evidence all by himself, the case is solved. Hagar does little during the last pages but stand and listen. Not her fault, but Hume's. To resolve the story, he lets the characters of the drama babble out all their secrets. Once caught in a lie, their mouths work incessantly. If they had stonewalled, no case would ever have been solved.

Two years pass. Hagar frets behind her cluttered counter. London sickens her. She dreams of bare-footed freedom and pots of garlic bubbling under forest trees. But not yet. Before the book can end, many loose strands must be drawn together. To make a beginning of that, we must first step back a few chapters to "The Seventh Customer and the Mandarin."

At that time, Hagar was assisted in the shop by the crippled boy, Bolker, one of fiction's least savory juveniles. A liar and thief, treacherous, quick minded, glib, Bolker has quickly picked up the rudiments of pawnbroking--although admittedly he is a dark stain on that necessary profession. Only Hume knows why Hagar saddled herself with such a disreputable assistant. First appearing in "The Crucifix," Bolker has a central role in "The Mandarin."

To compress ruthlessly, Larky Bill Smith, a thief, has concealed a stolen diamond necklace inside a Chinese Mandarin doll, just before he is arrested and carted off to gaol. Bolker discovers the diamonds and bolts with them. After Larky Bill is set free, he discovers that the diamonds are gone and charges off after Bolker. Finds him. Loses him. Is tricked by him.

Ultimately Vark learns that the police want Bill for the diamond theft, and promptly betrays that luckless felon for the reward. Bill swears he will return one day and chop Vark into small oblong bits.

As Bill is dragged foaming away, we learn that Bolker has returned the diamonds to their owner and collected a large reward.

So much for background. Now begins the final chapter, "The Passing of Hagar."

Enter the long lost Jimmy/Goliath. All this time he has been tucked neatly away in prison. But now he has returned to claim his inheritance. He remarks that Larky Bill has escaped and is rushing back to London to carve up Vark.

No sooner has Jimmy swaggered off to the pub than Eustace Lorn also reappears. He reports that, after years of searching, he met Jimmy on the road, just the other day, barely in time for the final chapter, and told him of the inheritance.

Eustace has not only located Jimmy but has made a success of himself. He has created a pretty business selling books from a caravan—a sort of closed, horse-drawn bookmobile—just as Roger Mifflin would do twenty years later in **Parnassus on Wheels**.

Flushed with success, Eustace proposes to Hagar. Her heart leaps. Losing every scrap of her common sense, she accepts him. In a mutual glow, they go to inspect the book wagon. Just in time to see a raggedy bum creep from inside and bolt away. Not to worry, Eustace says, It's merely a poor sick fellow he picked up en route. But Hagar has recognized Larky Bill.

All upset, she sends Eustace flying to advise Scotland Yard. She returns to the pawn shop to close her accounts and prepare to turn the business over to Jimmy. Nobody thinks of warning Vark, but you can't do everything at once.

Next morning, the business is transferred to Jimmy. Elated by thirty thousand pounds cash, he proposes to Hagar. Who rejects him in her usual outright manner:

> "Well, I won't marry you. I hate you!" cried Hagar, stamping her foot; "and indeed, if you must know, I'm going to marry Eustace Lorn."
>
> "What! That puppy," cried Jimmy in a rage.
>
> "That man—which you aren't! I'll live in a caravan and sell books."
>
> Here Jimmy broke out into imprecations, and was hardly restrained from violence, so enraged was he. He swore that for her years of service he would not give Hagar a penny; she would leave the pawn-shop as poor as when she entered it.
>
> "I intend to," said Hagar coolly. "I shan't even take the mourning I wore for your father. My red dress is good enough for the caravan of Eustace; and to-morrow I'll put it on, and leave the pawn-shop for ever."

You marvel that all this confrontational drama should be squandered in indirect discourse. A dime novel writer of the same period would have expanded it to two double-column pages of small type, mainly dialogue. But Hume is rather above that. Besides, he is hurtling toward a fine bloody accounting.

Vark has discovered that Jimmy is also an escaped convict and has notified the police. While stalling till they arrive, he makes an unsuccessful attempt to blackmail Jimmy of half the thirty thousand pounds. As they snarl at each other, Larky Bill bursts in with a knife. A fine to-do erupts.

Vark gets stabbed, then shot. Jimmy clutches vainly at Bill. The police lurch in. Bill twists away, plunges from the window to the river, and drowns.

That eliminates all immediate loose threads. Subsequently, Jimmy is pardoned, sells the pawn shop to Bolker (who buys it with his profits from the diamonds), and disappears.

As do Hagar and Eustace. Newly married and clinging tightly together, they mount the wagon, pass "down the lane, across the dancing shadows, and [ride] hopefully into the green country towards the gypsy life. Hagar of the Pawn-shop had come to her own at last."

Styles in heroines change nearly as rapidly as styles in fiction. Today Hagar. Tomorrow Madame Storey and Miss Marple. Next week, Modesty Blaise.

It is a long way back to those pre-1900 days, when the mystery story, unshaped and unsophisticated, was clawing its form from out of the air. More often than not, back in those remote days, the feminine detective need be only natural--a simple, untutored girl, quick minded and alert, who need only touch a problem to unravel it. She relied heavily on feminine intuition, a boon to the writer wishing relief from the heavy labor of constructing chains of evidence. And always a difficult romance hovered around her, never quite resolved until the final chapter. Then marriage terminated her brief career of detection.

These conventions later changed dramatically. As you note when reading cases of contemporary feminine detectives. But it was all different when Hagar tested her wits in that Lambeth pawn shop, so many generations ago.

Hagar is quaintly archaic now. Her creator, Hume, is nearly forgotten. But they remain embedded in literary history like ancient tree roots, clear evidence of how our present complexities have been nourished by the simplicities of the past.

(continued from page 36) delivers. Florence Ellredge plays the slatternly Ruby Lamar, wife of wrongly accused murderer. Irving Pichel, a pair of shady Southern poor whites who have a shred of decency, something you don't say about Larue. The claustrophic bordello sequences in which Temple submits to Trigger's sexual domination are effective, but the menacing, run-down house in the country where Temple is violated (with thunder and lightening to boot) smacks of B-film theatrics. In 1935, Pichel played the vampire's servant in **Dracula's Daughter**, a film in which sexual perversity was better--and more subtly--portrayed than in the 1933 film. So much for the Production Code of 1934. Or maybe horror films didn't count.

The films I have just discussed would not figure on my list of the Best Films of Cinevent 1985/1986, but--with the exception of the Gracie Allen/S.S. Van Dine concoction--were entertaining crime and melodrama films that may occasionally turn up on the late show. There was a time when I slept through those late showings. Now the Father's Day present of a VCR lets me sleep while an electronic eye shines in the dark and serenely records the films I have asked it to save for me. But that report will have to wait for another time.

Mickey Spillane's Mike Hammer: The Great Cover-Up

Jeff Banks

From its very onset, the telefilm and television series produced (and occasionally written) by Jay Bernstein has done a surprisingly good job of catching the ambience of Spillane's Hammer series books. The Spillane-Fellows theater release of 1963, **The Girl Hunters**, caught the magic still better, but, given the inherent differences between theater films and **anything** directly intended for TV, that would not be worth mentioning here except for the spectacular failure of the latest theater movie made from a Spillane book. The remake, more properly the second film version, of **I, the Jury**, was released the same year as the first Bernstein telefilm; both of these are available on videocassette, and seeing them close together should convince anyone of the superiority of the Bernstein product.

Another profitable comparison of **Mickey Spillane's Margin for Murder** (the first Bernstein telefilm) is with the latest, **The Return of Mickey Spillane's Mike Hammer**. Return received more advance publicity than any other telefilm, even exceeding that given most mini-series. Some of this was just Bernstein's capitalization of star Stacy Keach's drug conviction and serving time in England. But, as Paul Harvey is wont to say, wait until you hear **the rest of the story**.

A second major publicity source for **Return** was the idea that CBS-TV was going to use it as a "test" for possible resumption of the regular Hammer TV series. The honesty of the "test" idea is very questionable. Certainly CBS might well have decided **not** to resume the series this fall if **Return** had been a bomb, and it is equally true that any telefilm with characters suitable for a series is probably considered **at some point** as a trial balloon for a possible series, but the Hammer series had already had its trial runs, **and** it had been dropped in the first place only because Keach was unavailable. The likelihood is that the "test" aspect was nothing more than manufactured publicity.

Growing out of that was the business of "viewer demographics." The Hammer series had been **very** successful with men but had attracted few women viewers; that sounded good, but no source for the information--whether scientific viewer polling, crystal ball gazing, or whatever--was ever given. Yet it was trumpeted again and again that **Return** was going to be a "new look" Mike Hammer intended to appeal to a female audience without alienating the already satisfied male viewers.

Two format revisions were designed to accomplish this. First, **Return** would feature no bedroom scenes. Most of the Bernstein movies and TV episodes had shown the hero in bed with "the lady of the week"; these were not nearly so steamy as bedroom scenes on the soaps, but most evening TV dramas did not have bedroom scenes. Second, there would be no visual feast of all-but-bare breasts in this film; the episodes and the TV film featuring Keach as Hammer and Lindsay Bloom as Velda had developed women with well developed (and well displayed) upper torsos as an important trademark. In fact, Bloom could always be counted on to provide two major points of visual interest.

The most recent movie delivered on both promises. There was no bedroom scene, and breasts were very chastely covered (with two exceptions--the audience was showed the filming of police picking up prostitutes who were very lightly clad, which filming was to be a part of a feature movie whose star's little girl Hammer was protecting from a kidnapping; and the box office girl selling Hammer a ticket to see that movie in the final real scene of the show was dressed the way viewers had come to expect).

Whether or not such feminine charms as those of the Lite N' Easy barmaid will remain masked in the new season of episodes is a burning question that may be answered by the time you read this. Even if they do, the series should remain one of the better private eye efforts on the networks, and I am hopeful that it will remain as true to the character and ambience Spillane created with his books. In the books there was no emphasis upon breasts; Spillane fans have certainly not felt Bernstein's addition of that feature (those features?) was a violation of the Spillane milieu, but it is not essential to it.

From **Margin for Murder** onward, the Bernstein series has frequently emphasized the same sort of things Spillane did in the books. In that telefilm, Hammer's involvement grew from a desire to avenge a murdered friend (as in **I, the Jury** and a couple of other books in the series). There was tension between Hammer and his friend Pat Chambers, reminiscent of **The Girl Hunters**. While the ending sacrificed **personal** vengeance in favor of letting the law, public opinion, and Mafia associates do the punishing (and this was not Spillanian), there were other familiar elements. A highly trusted politician was one of the major villains as in **One Lonely Night**. Mafia involvement and smuggling (though of gems rather than drugs) harked back to **Kiss Me, Deadly**.

With the coming of Keach, the telefilms particularly seemed even closer in tune with what Spillane had written. **Murder Me, Murder You** featured a transvestite villain like Juno of **Vengeance Is Mine**, for instance. And the endings became more violent. Similarly, the TV episodes seemed more like the Spillane product than the old Darren McGavin TV series. This was especially apparent in the three rerun episodes directly following **Return** this spring. "A Bullet for Benny" featured a female villain as in **I, the Jury**, **The Big Kill** and others. "Shots in the Dark" and "Sex Trap" were both spy stories, which might seem a heavy emphasis for a private eye series until one remembers that **One Lonely Night, The Girl Hunters**, and **Survival Zero** are Hammer spy novels, that Spillane's only non-Hammer series (which featured Tiger Mann) was an espionage series, that of the non-series adult books **The Delta Factor** and **The Erection Set** feature spies as heroes and that there is a sprinkling of spy fiction in the several collections of shorter pieces.

As the "test" was originally announced, CBS claimed that **Return** and all three of these weekly reruns and audience reactions (in other words, ratings) would be considered before the network decided about the coming season. However, the decision to revive the series was announced **before** "Sex Trap" was aired, and it must have been made before rating results on "Shots in the Dark" were on the public record.

If "Shots" was any part of a "test," it was the perfect selection, as the teleplay by Larry Gross, Frank Abatemarco, Bill Froelich, and Mark Lisson (from Gross's original story) was a compendium of Spillane trademarks:

1. Hammer meets and befriends a girl in trouble who is soon killed, and he sets out to get justice for her. The situation is borrowed from **My Gun Is Quick**, where the victim was a prostitute, but the parallel between spying and prostitution (drawn even more explicitly in the following week in "Sex Trap") is an obvious one.

2. A spy secret capable of destroying America is the prize, as in **The Girl Hunters, Survival Zero,** and the final Tiger Mann book, **The By-Pass Control.**

3. Hammer makes bloody threats against the bad guys (and even some nominally good ones), as in virtually every Hammer book, and virtually every other Spillane hero does so in the other books.

4. Hammer gets into a more-or-less casual bar fight, as in at least half the books.

5. He insists (and convincingly proves) he has more freedom to do their job than the police, as is most emphatically demonstrated in **I, the Jury**, though it is seen in many of the other books as well.

6. An entertainer passes the hero vital information after exchange of a musical code-word, as in the non-series book, **The Delta Factor.**

7. Hammer picks up an important clue from a body in the morgue, as in **Kiss Me, Deadly.** This was also prominent in **Return.**

8. The emphasis on nostalgia, which permeates the TV series more heavily than it does the Spillane books, is even more pronounced than is usual, with references to Saturday matinees (movies) and Forties' pop music.

9. The familiar Spillane target, an unfeeling bureaucracy, greatly agitates Hammer. This is a factor in at least half the Hammer books and all of Spillane's others dealing with spying, but it is not confined just to that majority.

10. The major villain is again revealed to be a female, as in **I, the Jury**, etc.

11. The villain meets a super-violent end in a vat of bubbling chemicals. Only two or three of Spillane's adult books lack this sort of ending. However, for the TV audience's benefit, she was shown a bedraggled and thoroughly embarrassed survivor at the end. The series does not always provide spectacular comeuppances for the villains, but on the other hand they don't always survive super-violent finishes, either.

The appearance of the third rerun episode, "Sex Trap," was made somewhat redundant by the announcement, some forty-eight hours before the broadcast, that the series had been reinstated for Fall 1986. This original teleplay by a frequent writer for the series, B.W. Sandefur, reworked several Spillane concerns frequently seen in the spy stories and episodes, but it also covered some territory not explored in "Shots." For instance, Hammer learns that an old girlfriend is a U.S. spy, as with Velda in **The Girl Hunters**; there is an emphasis on hidden-camera blackmail, as in **Vengeance Is Mine**; poetic justice is emphasized in the hero's use of the KGB mastermind's own blackmail scheme to destroy him (poetic justice being a device seen in most Spillane books); diplomatic immunity is a target of Hammer's invective, as in **The Body Lovers**; the UN is excoriated, albeit somewhat more lightly than in the first Tiger Mann book, **Day of the Guns.**

Another announced revision of **Return** was a "new" emphasis on the gentle side of Hammer, making his feeling for the little girl marked for kidnapping the real reason for his participation in her case. In the Hammer books that gentle side is displayed several times in **I, the Jury** in his concern for his murdered friend's fiancee, and it appears in virtually all the books. However, in many of them (and even more frequently in the various visual Hammers) the objects of his compassion happen to be beautiful women; he would be something less than human to view them with unmixed motives. This makes it easy for those who read or view casually (and that includes most "critics," as I have maintained elsewhere) or for those with an axe to grind to misread his motivation.

After **I, the Jury** and excluding beautiful women, Hammer's human compassion was expressed in the books toward an infant orphan in **The Big Kill**, another war buddy in **Vengeance Is Mine**, a teenaged girl orphan (but those prone to disagree with me will insist he has a "dirty old man" letch for her) in **The Snake**, a boy who has been used as a laboratory animal in psychological experimentation in **The Twisted Thing**, and this is to ignore secondary objects of his compassion. In the first season the Keach TV episodes feature him helping an old couple who had been swindled, so his instant conquest by the six-year-old in **Return** is not a new character development, but merely a characteristic that had been underdisplayed in the past.

Such compassionate humanity is, of course, a characteristic straight out of the pulp detectives, undeniably the source of the Hammer character to begin with.

Finally, even when he rushes to the aid of a beautiful woman, as in "Shot in the Dark," any hero but Hammer would be viewed with a certain amount of charity.

After all, despite the obligatory compliment by her superior after she is dead, "better than any man in my unit," echoed in almost the exact words by the superior of the severely injured (and hospitalized) female spy in "Sex Trap," and despite any extravagant claims made by women's liberation advocates, few people would seriously suggest that an unarmed woman would need no help against two armed and well trained men.

Even the TV Spencer, who spends more than half of every episode in his three favorite activities (quoting poetry, searching his soul, and being helped by Hawk), rushes most often to the aid of pretty women. If this is macho sexism when Hammer does it, then why not when others do? Simply because in every case, **including Hammer**, what it really is is writers cleverly getting multiple values out of a dramatic situation in order to heighten its drama.

(continued from page 28) of again.

The statement that went with "ten" in the code books then in use was "Grandfather has fixed the roof." Under the circumstances, the statement was meaningless. London decided that the French agent had only been holding her hands out asking for help.

Twenty or so years afterward, the Englishman who had been the French agent's contact, still sure there had been some unheeded message in her ten up-raised fingers and haunted by his memory of the incident, told Griswold about it.

As Griswold said as he began, "Concepts are not, in any case, universal. A difference in language can alter a concept"--in this case, the English and the French concepts of "Ten."

The Rural Policeman in American Mystery Fiction

George Dove

The rural policeman has never figured as prominently in the work of the mystery writers of the United States as in those of England, partly because the characteristically American hard-boiled story has tended toward an urban setting and partly because American writers have never shared the English fondness for the lethal week-end party at a remote country house, where the local rustics have a chance to bumble about for a few pages before calling in the Yard.

His relative scarcity may be the reason why he has never been conventionalized in the American mystery. He may conform to the type of the canny, homespun rube, like "Chief" Forrest, the one-man police force of Chilton, New York, in Lawrence Sanders' **The First Deadly Sin.** Captain Edward X. Delaney, one of the most overbearing of big city cops, finds it necessary to enlist the help of "Chief" Forrest in tracking down a fugitive. To the secret delight of all of Delaney's subordinates, the rustic cop promptly and thoroughly puts Delaney in his place, addressing him as "Sonny" and otherwise keeping him reminded whose territory he is encroaching on. The American rural policeman is occasionally lazy and incompetent, like the official dunderheads in Hammett's **Dain Curse**, who are always underfoot when the Continental Op is about to make a little progress in the case. Very rarely is he as completely isolated from the twentieth century as Sheriff Courtney Clock of Rutland County, Pennsylvania, in one of the Frank Sessions novels of Hillary Waugh. Sessions, a New York City cop, calls the sheriff in connection with a missing person complaint, and he has difficulty in pinning Clock down to a discussion of the case in hand because the sheriff can't stop expressing wonder over the fact that there is one whole squad of detectives in Manhattan who handle nothing but homicides; after a few minutes of this, the sheriff tells Sessions it is time to milk the cows, and hangs up in his face. He is sometimes a brutal petty tyrant, like the Montana Sheriff Haight in Rex Stout's **Death of a Dude**, who at one point makes the mistake of trying to over-ride Nero Wolfe. Wolfe tells him to shut up; he does. He is more likely, especially in the recent stories, to be a competent professional, like Sheriff Daryl Tice in Rex Burns' **Avenging Angel**, who organizes the desert ambush of a criminal gang with the skill of a military strategist. Or, he may be short on professionalism but long on competence, like Captain Slocum in Hillary Waugh's **Madam Will Not Dine Tonight**, who can at least recognize superior ability and lends a hand to the private investigator, who successfully solves the crime. Whatever his category, the American rural cop is not a stereotype.

He does, though, show a tendency toward certain

characteristics that distinguish him from the city cop in fiction. He is much more likely to personalize a situation and to think in terms of individual relationships rather than broad societal principles. Hugh Holman's South Carolina Sheriff John Macready puts the point well when he says, "I hate these things.... Diggin' into people's lives, stirrin' up trouble. 'Tain't much fun.." With them, compassion often takes precedence over the rule-book, as it does with Janwillem van de Wetering's Maine sheriff, who holds a local drunk in jail until he can send some prisoners over to cut firewood for him so he will not freeze when he goes home. One personal ability of these rural cops is their skill with the put-down. A moment ago I mentioned "Chief" Forrest's practice of addressing Captain Delaney as "Sonny"; most of them, as a matter of fact, call all younger men "son," and Burns' Sheriff Tice accomplishes the squelch of a pushy Denver reporter named Gargan by persistently calling him "Mr. Gargle" over the phone.

Their tendency to personalize represents the sharpest contrast between the rural cops and their city counterparts, a predictable by-product of the de-personalization of urban life. The city policeman in fiction is quite capable of sympathy toward criminals and the victims of crime, but his motives are different: he is not likely to have family ties with the people he deals with professionally (as the rural cops frequently do) or to come into contact with any of them socially.

A second distinguishing quality is the inclination of the rural policeman to think and act almost exclusively in terms of the locality. This tendency takes two forms. The rural cop usually knows his territory like a book, and he is expert in application of local knowledge. "I just naturally know every man, woman, child, and hound dog in these parts," says Sheriff Macready, and he does not exaggerate. In **The First Deadly Sin** Edward X. Delaney decides it is time to shake "Chief" Forrest and tells the "Chief" he will find his way unaided through the rough terrain where the fugitive is holed up. Forrest is disgusted: "That's the first dumb thing you've said, sonny," he tells Delaney. Quite often their knowledge of the locality simply permits them to adapt to circumstances they would not ordinarily condone. Gabriel Wager of the Denver Police Department quickly notices that Sheriff Tice's office is riddled with nepotism, but he reflects that this is good politics on Tice's part and one way of assuring an adequate budget for his department. More to the point, though, is their habit of putting the local welfare above all other loyalties. In Lillian O'Donnell's **Cop Without a Shield**, Norah Mulcahaney of the New York Police Department is appalled by the way Chief Blegen, of York Crossing, Pennsylvania, knowingly permits an illegal industry to operate in his territory; Blegen finally admits to her that he entered into the local conspiracy of silence because of the financial benefit the factory has brought to the town.

In their tendency to think in terms of locality, the rural police are not too different from their city colleagues. It is not unusual for a city detective in fiction to know every square inch of his precinct or every member of every street gang. The big difference between them lies in the rural policeman's protective attitude toward the welfare of the local community. When she discovers the operation of the factory that employs illegal immigrant labor, Norah Mulcahaney, a thoroughly professional city policewoman, can think only in terms of the flagrant violation of the law represented by the operation, and the death of the young Mexican woman who was killed in the process of a coverup. Chief Blegen, though, must think in terms of the local welfare: "The town is dying," he tells Norah. "The loss of sixty jobs ... will be a severe blow."

The third special quality of the country cop is his inclination to simplify, to reduce things to basics, to take short cuts, to approach all situations at a minimum level of formality. To a lawyer who complains that his methods are "most irregular," Sheriff Macready replies, "I ain't never been famous for regularity." Nor are most of them. Captain Delaney, at the state park where the fugitive is holed up, needs to make a phone call and is annoyed to find the park headquarters locked. "Chief" Forrest is not in the least disturbed; he draws his gun and unconcernedly shoots the lock off the door. The best illustration of their skill at simplification, though, is the statement made by one of them of a basic principle of detective fiction. You may remember how Dupin put it in "The Murders in the Rue Morgue": "It appears to me that this mystery is considered insoluble, for the very reason which should cause it to be regarded as easy of solution—I mean for the outre character of its features." Now listen to a statement of the same idea by Constable Jim Patton in Raymond Chandler's *Lady in the Lake*: "I ought to of thought of it myself. But if I had, it would be one of those ideas a fellow would throw away almost as quick as he thought of it. It would look to kind of far-fetched."

At one level, city cops tend to reduce things to basics and take short cuts to as great a degree as the rustics do, but as a general rule the city detective goes by the book. for his own protection. The biggest difference between him and his rural counterpart lies in the casual attitude of the country cop. When the state police try to take him to task for destroying state property, "Chief" Forrest's reply is, "O Lord, will my afflictions never cease?" The rural policeman is, naturally, subject to less organization, and hence less standardization than the urban cop.

Before we leave the subject of the rural cop in mystery fiction, we should at least mention the most recent development, the figure of the former city policeman who now works in a rural setting. In Rex Burns' latest novel there is a country detective who has moved from a California town to rural Colorado in order to get away from a police force where little energy was expended on training and quite a bit on bleeding traffic fines out of the tourist population. Chief Blegen, in the O'Donnell novel, is a veteran of the Philadelphia police department who settled in York Crossing in the hope of finding "a calm place, with little corruption and less violence." It may be that, as the stress of city life continues to grow in intensity, we will meet more of these former city cops in rural settings in mystery stories.

I remarked at the beginning of this discussion that the rural cop in mystery fiction is no stereotype. Neither is he an anomaly. He is in a very direct sense the personification of his community's attitude toward law enforcement and its need for security. The sheriff in the Nero Wolfe story is a petty tyrant because of the indifference of the local populace. The ambivalence of Chief Blegen in the Norah Mulcahaney story is a reflection of the ambivalence of the people of York Crossing, who want law and order but also economic security. Sometimes the rural policeman is a buffer between the peaceful, genteel folk of his community and the hard realities of the wicked world. In the Rex Burns novel, a pious citizen remarks to Sheriff Tice that "[man's] soul is eternal." "Let the good Lord look after the souls," Tice replies. "My job is to look after the flesh."

Scandinavian Mystery Scene

K Arne Blom

In 1977 I wrote an article in Dilys Winn's Edgar-winning **Murder Ink** about the Swedish police procedural mystery. Almost ten years have gone since then--and what has happened during this decade?

Well, first of all, in 1977 the mystery in Sweden was a very big market. During the seventies more mysteries by Swedish writers were published than ever before, and the output of translations from primarily the U.S. and England was enormous. But that wasn't all. Books from France, Denmark, Czechoslovakia (to name a few countries) were translated in a number like never before. And on top of that, five special series of mysteries especially chosen by experts were published. In those series both new books and old classic ones never before translated were seeing print in the Swedish tongue.

The popularity of the mystery was enormous. But the situation today is quite different. The mystery is a rather small genre in Sweden, compared to those days. Fewer Swedish writers are writing and being published, and fewer and fewer books are being translated. That the translations published are fewer is nothing to feel too sorry about. During the heydays it went too far. Too many lousy books by too many not-too-talented foreign mystery writers were published. It was as if the publishers had to publish mysteries and not give a damn about the quality as long as they were able to put out mysteries and thrillers.

As a matter of fact, it was the thriller that was biggest. Sweden has had very few good writers of thrillers. The number of good thrillers written by Swedish (or Scandinavian) writers are easily counted on one hand's fingers. But we had an avalanche of American and English thrillers translated. The publication of Frederic Forsyth's **The Day of the Jackal** created a great interest in the international thriller, and we had the good ones in translation; but, alas, also too many of the really stinking bad ones.

What was big in Sweden--and Scandinavia--during those good years was also the police procedural mystery. Per Wahloo and Maj Sjowall had written their ten books about Martin Beck and his working colleagues. They had been translated into many languages. They were even awarded an Edgar. Their world fame created an international interest in the Scandinavian mystery, and there were some Danish and Swedish writers who were published in English, Russian, Italian, and about in every language in the world.

It has never been said, but hinted at, that Wahloo-Sjowall owed a great deal to Ed McBain. According to Per they didn't know about McBain when they started to work on their own series of ten police procedurals. They were, said Per to me once, influenced by John Creasey's books written as J.J. Marric about Gideon.

When talking to Ed McBain one gets the feeling that he is somewhat irritated over his Swedish colleagues Wahloo-Sjowall for imitating. Well, one doesn't have to read McBain and get influence for writing police procedurals. It seems today that McBain is about the only writer in the world who is great in the genre. But let's not forget that Hillary Waugh long before McBain wrote books that must still today be considered as the best police procedurals ever written—and that before him Lawrence Treat invented the genre and brought it to perfection. And there were others: the Gordons, Ben Benson, Thomas Walsh.

Anyhow, somewhere Per and Maj got the idea and inspiration for a series of books—and created a real masterpiece in ten parts. And when I wrote that article for Dilys' book back in 1977, I could tell about Jacob Palme, Olle Hogstrand, Olov Svedelid, Kjell E. Genberg and myself also writing about policemen. I could have added the Norwegian writer Tor Edvin Dahl, who under the pen name David Torjussen wrote well-worth-reading police procedurals. And the Dane Poul-Henrik Trampe, who did a very fine series of books. The Danish writer Torben Nielsen was translated and published in both the U.S. and England. His last four books in the genre—none in translation—showed him as a forceful and important writer. In those he dealt with contemporary items in a very realistic manner and created memorable books about policemen, victims, and criminals. This ex-policeman doesn't write any more. He was killed in a car crash a couple of years ago. And Trampe doesn't write any more. He drowned under mysterious circumstances during a boat trip from Copenhagen to Oslo. And as far as I know, Dahl doesn't write about policemen any more.

In Sweden, Palme stopped writing years ago, Hogstrand did too, Svedelid has killed off his police hero and Genberg wrote three police procedurals in all. There are a couple of newcomers, Uno Palmstrom and Lena Holfve, but neither of them is worth much attention. Holfve was the first woman to write police procedurals, but also proved to be the least talented writer. Leif G.W. Persson made himself a name writing three books, of which one is a memorable police novel about the investigation of the murder of a prostitute. This was his second police procedural. The first was rather promising and the last one somewhat overworked, ending up as too much of an idea novel and too little as a novel about people.

There is at least one writer of police procedurals in Finland, Matti Joensuu, like the late Nielsen also an ex-policeman. I have read one of his books, and it didn't create any wish to read more.

So that is the status of the police procedural mystery in Scandinavia of today—it isn't much to brag about. As for myself, I am publishing one this fall and that will probably be my last. Frankly, as a writer one gets somewhat bored of the formula and the limitations. I will enter another field of the mystery—having become aware that one reaches a limit from where it is very difficult to work on and find new ways in trying to create interesting plots. The police procedure one has to describe from book to book is very much alike. There is a certain limit one reaches and after that one feels that one is finished with this particular kind of mystery. The urge to move on to other kinds of books becomes too great and irresistible.

Communicating with friends in the U.S. and England I have learned that after some bad years the mystery is big again. It is a fact that when it comes to books we are some two, three years after the trends in the U.S. and England. So my guess is that the genre will bloom again in Scandinavia, with all the interesting and good factors this means. Slowly the mystery in this part of the world is waking up from its long sleep. And, interesting enough, the new trend and wave seems to be the hardboiled mystery.

Gunnar Staalesen and Kim Smage in Norway have written very popular and very good hardboiled mysteries. Smage is a woman, which is extra interesting; the first Scandinavian woman to write hardboiled. In Denmark we have Dan Turell, who so far is the Scandinavian master of the hardboiled.

In Sweden we are still waiting for the first writer of good hardboiled mysteries.

Reading the books by our new Scandinavian hardboiled writers, one realizes that you don't have to write about back alleys in New York or mean streets in Los Angeles to create interesting and fascinating hardboiled mysteries.

I claimed some ten years ago that in Scandinavia wrote and worked at least eight mystery writers well worth being translated and published in the U.S. and England, and that three or four of them were as good as the best writers in those countries. Staalesen, Smage, and Turell are as good as many an English or American mystery writer.

My guess is that the hardboiled school will flourish as never before very soon--and I hope that the world will keep an eye on what will happen in the Scandinavian countries. There will come many interesting books from this side of the mystery scene.

(continued from page 33) He was something of a joke in his own lifetime because he propounded so many unusual theories. He was sure there were many variations of man in the world, some who were ape-like, some who were born with only one leg, and others with goat's feet. He also thought, based on his reading of **The Iliad**, that Achilles had been more than fourteen feet tall. Possessor of great wealth, Monboddo was alleged to be carrying out experiments to convert his gold into more "useful" metals like iron and tin.

In Lillian de la Torre's story the unconventional ideas of Monboddo are contrasted with the logical mind of Samuel Johnson. Occasionally, Monboddo comes off as being ahead of his time. Unlike Johnson, he was a great believer in bathing (though he was wont to do so outdoors, regardless of temperature). He was also a vegetarian, while Johnson favored rare roast beef. De la Torre's Watson, Boswell, narrates how during their stay a wild boy, said to be living in the trees, is brought to the estate. Monboddo sees this as an opportunity to prove his hypotheses; Johnson sees the situation as a mystery to be solved. The resulting blend of fact and fiction is one of the most delightful stories in what Anthony Boucher called "the best series of historical mysteries ever written."

The Cream of Queen

Frank Floyd

When, earlier this year, I wrote to those TMFers who had contributed to the magazine in the past and asked them to send me material for this issue, Frank Floyd responded with the proposal that he do a regular column, under the title "The Cream of Queen," in which he would highlight what he considered to be the best short story which appeared in the two (sometimes three) issues of EQMM which would appear between each bi-monthly appearance of TMF. I replied that I wasn't sure whether the readership would be all that interested in a review of a short story, and that, furthermore, TMF was getting a bit top-heavy with columns already, what with regular appearances by Marv Lachman and Walter Albert, in addition to the editorial column, which has been known to run on at great length. But I agreed to give it a try, and Frank has turned in two columns to date--for May-June and for July-August--which I have combined into one. Frank and I would like to have your comments on the column so that we can decide whether to make it a regular feature, run it irregularly as space permits, of drop the idea altogether. GMT.

Clark Howard, "The Last One to Cry," EQMM, June 1986.

June's **Ellery Queen's Mystery Magazine** has more good stories than any issue I can recall. There is the latest Nick Velvet story (Velvet, the most original of Edward D. Hoch's many creations, steals only worthless objects). There is Isaac Asimov's fifty-third Black Widowers tale, which gives an account of how the Black Widowers help a noted historian acquire a set of books--a subject which strikes to the heart of bibliophiles like myself—and which also gives lessons in history and geography within a mystery as logical as Dr. Asimov's own **Realm of Algebra** except for $2x^0$ slight errors. There is James Powell's tale about a Canadian Mountie who spends a night in the estate house of two families of congenital loonies who have intermarried over the years and produced even loonier offspring. Has any other persevering minion of the law ever been chloroformed and stapled to the door of the library? It turns out to be a very confining place from which to conduct an investigation.

In "The Last One to Cry" Clark Howard has produced a Halley's comet of a short story--short stories which keep you turning pages as if they were 80,000 word potboilers don't appear much more often than that fabled comet. Martin and Loop and Freddy Walsh were once one-for-and-all-all-for-one buddies; that was when they and some other boys were in reform school together. Now Martin has a responsible position as a personnel manager for a large paper-products firm, a bright future, and an affectionate wife and family who depend on him and have faith in him as husband and father. He is the only one of the reform school group to make good in the outside world and become an asset rather than a debit to society. One day Old Man Mackay comes to the paper-products firm looking for a job. Mackay is the man who killed Freddy Walsh. Martin and Loop had sworn to each other than one of them would get Mackay some day, and Martin is determined to keep his promise.

I might have told Mr. Clark Howard that his telling his story by switching back and forth between the past and present would cause it to end up as a series of disconnected scenes, as dozens of stories I could name have ended up. But I'd have been wrong. His transitions from past to present, past to present, slip by unnoticed, which is a remarkable accomplishment. Howard escapes the pitfalls of modern fiction. "The Last One to Cry" attains reality without crudeness; it depicts human feelings and emotions without bathos or nihilism; it holds the reader's interest without vulgarity or bizarrerie or barbarism; and it makes a statement without author intrusion or self-important stylistic experimentation, either of which interfere with telling what happens to the characters. Let those who claim all mystery is escape literature compare their favorite so-called serious story with "The Last One to Cry." Beware of the ending: it seems to be handing you sweetness, only to take it back and slap you in the face.

Isaac Asimov, "Ten," EQMM, August 1986.

Depending on the criteria used in judging them, seven other July-August stories could be rated equal to or better than "Ten." All seven are superior to it in characterization. Everything considered, for the most all-around entertaining and readable of the lot, 'Scalplock," by Clark Howard, would probably have the edge.

"Ten," however, is the best done puzzle mystery I have come across in many long days. In this type of mystery too much direct characterization can be diverting from the puzzle, which is the main reason for the reader's interest, but the author himself has to know his characters thoroughly, make them fit the part, and keep them consistent, and he should also provide the reader with an understanding of the relevant abilities and foibles of the puzzle-solver. Of course, well chosen, unobtrusive, short, and distinct character descriptions or details in the manner of Sir Arthur Conan Doyle are generally a big plus, even in the puzzle mystery.

The puzzle-solver in "Ten" is Griswold, an employee of the Department in Washington and long since more or less cast into outer darkness there for being right and saying so too often. In the summer of 1942, just before the Allied commando raid on Dieppe, a grim fiasco in which half the Allied force was taken prisoner or killed, a beautiful French spy was captured by the German Gestapo. As she was being led away, there was enough moonlight for her to see and recognize her contact, a young Englishman, passing by on a bicycle. She held up both hands and signaled "ten"; he saw her fingers extended, clearly, all ten of them. Her fate at the hands of the Gestapo was only a matter of conjecture. She was never heard

(Continued on page 20.)

IT'S ABOUT CRIME
by Marvin Lachman

While TMF was away there were some interesting developments in the mystery, too many to cover except in highlight form. Mysteries have become "in," and some of the most popular weekly television shows are in our field, most notably a genuine whodunit, **Murder, She Wrote**, starring Angela Lansbury. **Moonlighting** is the kind of Private Eye show you either love or hate. The plots have the consistency of wet tissue, but there is witty dialogue and some of the funniest slapstick I've ever seen on the small tube. Police procedurals remain reasonably popular with **Cagney and Lacey** and **Hill Street Blues**, the latter making many changes to try (not yet successfully) to maintain its stature. A little less soap and a bit more detection would help.

The current state of mystery short story magazines indicates a trend away from the general toward the specialized. **Mike Shayne Mystery Magazine** died the death that its contributors who had so much trouble getting paid expected. A revival of **The Saint Mystery Magazine** only lasted three issues before going into oblivion. However, **Espionage** is into its second year and is a good mixture of short stories, articles, and interviews. In short story length, parodies of spy fiction (especially by Ron Goulart) have worked better than more serious spy fiction. Information is available at P.O. Box 48000, Bergenfield, NJ 07621.

Two magazines have come along which specialize in tough fiction. The slicker of the two is **The New Black Mask**, from Harcourt, Brace, Jovanovich, which recently published its fifth issue. Priced at $7.95, it is available in many book stores. After starting out unpromisingly with too many excerpts from published or to-be-published novels plus a new Jim Thompson novel which was unwisely serialized over **four** issues, NBM is becoming what it should be: a trade paperback devoted mainly to short stories, with the occasional interview. Most of the authors are established, but they have not been afraid to publish newcomers, e.g., James O'Keefe, with a promising debut regarding a psychiatrist detective.

HARDBOILED is what its name implies, and its appeal has been to people who like that type of fiction and don't mind seeing the boundaries of taste tested, if not actually broken. There are articles and even tough poetry, but short stories are the nucleus here, too. Two very early efforts by the now popular Max Allan Collins have proved interesting, if raw. Better stories have been by Robert Randisi, Paul Bishop, Ed Gorman, and the editor/publisher, Wayne Dundee, from whom information about **Hardboiled** can be obtained at 903 #8 W. Jackson St., Belvidere, IL 61008.

There has been no dearth of material **about** the mystery.

including two trade paperbacks to add to the immense library of Sherlockiana. Michael Hardwick, one of the most knowledgeable of all regarding the Master, has written a fictional biography: **Sherlock Holmes: My Life and Crimes** ($7.95 from Henry Holt). Here are some outstanding scholarship, excellent turn of the century photographs, and a great cover evoking the London of Doyle's times. Also illustrated with Baker Street photographs is a Penguin book, **Letters to Sherlock Holmes** ($6.95), a collection of interesting and amusing letters written to the most famous character in all of literature.

John Breen's Edgar winner for 1984, **Novel Verdicts: A Guide to Courtroom Fiction**, from Scarecrow Press, 52 Liberty St., P.O. Box 656, Metuchen, NJ 08840 ($18.50 in hardcover), tells everything one could want to know about legal mysteries, whetting the reader's appetite, yet never disclosing more than is necessary. Mysteries about the law are practically the only subject omitted (and with Breen's book we did not need it) from **The Subject is Murder: A Selective Subject Guide to Mystery Fiction**, by Albert J. Menedez, published in hardcover by Garland Publishing Co., 136 Madison Ave., New York, NY 10016, at $25. The book contains lists of mysteries about such varied topics as Advertising, Libraries, Music, Sports, and Christmas--twenty-five in all. A second edition of **Twentieth Century Crime and Mystery Writers** has been published by St. Martin's, 175 Fifth Ave., New York, NY 10010, at $69.95, adding many new writers who have come on the scene since the first edition in 1980. A few writers were injudiciously omitted, but then space was a consideration, even in a book that runs 1,094 pages of critical articles, factual biographies, and complete bibliographical data for hundreds of writers. It's one of the indispensable reference books for mystery fans.

Finally, lest the editor/publisher of the journal you are now reading be too modest to mention it, his Brownstone Books had themselves an Edgar winner, my fellow columnist, Walter Albert, for **Mystery and Detective Fiction: An International Bibliography of Secondary Sources**, 779 incredibly useful and accurate pages regarding material about the mystery, priced at $60 and worth every penny.

Because literally hundreds of new mystery novels, as well as reprints, have appeared during the last two years, space would not permit me to cover all of them, even if I had had the time to read them. However, there are some I want to recommend and others I want to warn readers against so that if their reading tastes are in "sync" with mine, they will be spared time and expense.

Lawrence Block, **Deadly Honeymoon** (Jove, $2.95). Transplant Cornell Woolrich into a more permissive decade, and you would have this book, first published as a paperback original in 1967. A young attorney and his bride go to a remote Pennsylvania cabin for their honeymoon, but it is interrupted by rape and murder. In this brutal but extremely suspenseful novel, a manhunt is generated by a desire for revenge with which the reader can easily identify.

John Dickson Carr, **The Emperor's Snuff-Box** (Carroll & Graf, $3.50). This book is best described by quoting Carr, himself, regarding the murder in it: "This is a domestic crime. A cozy, comfortable, hearth-rug murder." Though not the author at his best, this is typical Carr. There is love at first sight, and the setting is France, though most of the characters are British. There is less atmosphere than usual, and the puzzle is a bit less complicated, and, therefore, more guessable, than most Carrs. None of Carr's usual series characters are present; the murder is investigated by a French policeman and a vacationing British psychiatrist. The time is the summer of 1939 and the delight of a simpler time and an intriguing puzzle make this worthwhile, even if it is not Carr at his peak.

Anne Chamberlain, **The Tall Dark Man** (Academy Chicago, $4.95). The plot of this 1955 mystery, reprinted in an especially attractive edition, is decidedly Woolrichian. A thirteen year-old girl says she has seen a murder through the window of her Ohio school room, but no one will believe her. She also claims that the murderer saw and recognized **her**. When Anthony Boucher originally reviewed this book, he paid it the extravagant praise of saying "This is purely and absolutely, The Suspense Novel, in an ideal form, which the genre rarely attains." He did not exaggerate very much.

Kate Gallison, **Unbalanced Accounts** (Little, Brown, hardcover, $14.95). A promising first novel turns out to be ultimately disappointing. The setting is unusual, a decaying area of Trenton where private detective Nicholas Magaracz has been hired by the New Jersey Bureau of Mental Rehabilitation to investigate the theft of 375 checks. There is very little else in the way of plot or characterization to justify this book. Most of the people are indistinguishable. Those who aren't are so unbelievable or obnoxious as to cause reader apathy. There's a good mystery in the inner working of a large state bureaucracy, but this isn't it.

Andrew Garve, **The Ascent of D-13** and **Two if by Sea** (Perennial Library, $3.50 each). It's good to see Garve being reprinted, and these two books, published almost two decades apart, will serve as a splendid introduction to a writer who wrote more than thirty novels, no two of which seem cut from the same pattern. The only similarity in these two books is that both are about the Cold War and both are genuinely exciting and suspenseful. In **The Ascent of D-13** (1968), rival Western and Russian mountain climbers "race" up a rugged peak on the Turkish-Armenian border to recapture a secret weapon on a plane which has crashed. **Two if by Sea**, which Garve originally published in 1949 as by Roger Bax, grabs the reader quickly with its tale of a British correspondent's efforts to rescue his Russian wife from behind the Iron Curtain. Garve's effective use of a sailing background is a bonus.

Nicholas Guild, **Chain Reaction** (Berkley, $3.95). Forget you know the results of World War II. This is one of those books in which the author wants you to guess whether Herman Goering will throw out the first ball at the 1946 World Series. Actually, it starts out well enough as, in January 1944, an anti-Nazi, but loyal, German officer is landed in New England on a mission which can possibly save Hitler's beleaguered war effort. The early chapters are quite good, but then evidence of careless writing and poor research (frequent anachronisms) creep in. There is a switch in character focus midway which weakens things even further, so that by the end we really don't care how the book will end. Incidentally, this was a book with **eleven** swastikas on the cover. That, alone, should have deterred me from reading it.

Michael Innes, **The Daffodil Affair** (Penguin, $3.50) and **The Weight of the Evidence** (Perennial Library, $2.95). These books, originally published in 1942 and 1943 respectively, come from the most imaginative period in the career of this writer who has been publishing mysteries for **fifty** years. **Daffodil** is probably too wild and improbable for its own good, as we are asked to believe, on the basis of flimsy evidence, that Appleby and another Scotland Yard inspector would be sent out of war-time London into the jungles of South America. The story begins attractively with the stolen titular horse and is heavy on human and animal psychology, accurately using the famous "Hans Legacy" about teaching horses tricks. Finally, there is too little action and too unlikely an ending to justify what is otherwise an unusual and sophisticated book. **The Weight of the Evidence** is relatively conventional for Innes, with its British university setting immediately before World War II, but it opens with an unpopular professor found crushed to death by a **meteor**. It's all very clever, but sometimes the literary allusions and sheer number of eccentric characters is a bit overdone. There's a lot of good detection, though it is weakened by too much coincidence and a fortuitous confession at the end.

Jonathan Kellerman, **When the Bough Breaks** (Signet, $3.95). This Edgar-winner for Best First Mystery Novel of 1985 reads like a private eye novel, though its protagonist is a child psychologist. Kellerman believes in letting a simile be his narrator's umbrella, tossing in lines like: "The sky was as cold and hard as a handgun." He also is given to use of trendy plot devices: child molesting, homosexuality, and car chases. Now that I've told you its weaknesses, I can proceed to recommend this book as extremely readable, with an interesting plot and many characters about whom you'll care. Psychologists and psychiatrists are well depicted by one who knows. (Mr. K. is a child psychologist himself.) He also knows Los Angeles, and few recent books have captured as many aspects of life in that city as this does.

Sefton Kyle, **Guilty, But—** (Herbert Jenkins, 1927). After you've had your dose of current pathology in a book like Kellerman's, it is a pleasure to read something as delightfully old-fashioned as this book which Roy Vickers wrote under the Kyle pseudonym. Here is a book with old-fashioned virtues and old-fashioned plot devices. Connie Elmore finds a body, but it is gone when she brings back the police, and they refuse to believe her. The more she tells her story, the less she is believed, and she soon feels "as if she were playing a part in her own nightmare." She, of necessity, turns amateur detective and finds herself competing with Detective-Inspector Rason who Vickers would feature as part of his excellent Department of Dead Ends series. A less credible plot than Vickers usually presented is helped immeasurably by his underrated narrative skill. Here's a book worth reprinting, just the thing for the imaginative editors at Harper's Perennial Library.

Warren Murphy, **Trace** (Signet $2.95). "Trace" is a renaming of the character, "Digger," of another paperback original series before Murphy fell out with Pocket Books. I didn't care for "Digger" and was perfectly prepared to dislike him as "Trace." He's a graduate of the smart-ass school of detectives, sounding like David Addison on **Moonlighting**, but not having Maddie Hayes to play off. Murphy follows a current trend by making Trace and his girl friend combine as many adjectival groups as possible. His hero is an Irish-Jewish alcoholic; Trace's girl friend, Chico, is a Japanese-Italian card dealer (with a college degree) and part-time hooker. Trace has an abiding hatred for his ex-wife, his children, and his mother, but none of these are explained. Whatever happened to real eccentricity, as in Holmes or Wolfe? Yet, though Trace is not keener than most persons, in this book his creator really allows him to function as a detective with an interesting case involving lawyers and possible murder at a nursing home. Eventually we start to like Trace a bit and to enjoy his lines. By the time the book is over, we have had a good time; well, at least, I did, and I think you will, too. If you like Trace, there are now five more books about him since this one launched the series in 1983.

Raymond Postgate, **Verdict of Twelve** (Academy Chicago, $4.95). Few books after this 1940 effort have used the device of a jury "solving" a murder mystery. (Exception: the television play/movie, **Twelve Angry Men**). Postgate did it so well that he practically broke the mold. The idea of a collective detective, consisting of a dozen people, remains inherently fascinating since this is, after all, the function of a jury. Postgate succeeded in making his jury (or at least most of them) really come alive as they deliberate and weigh the evidence in a trial of a woman accused of poisoning her nephew. Not the least interesting part of the book is the prejudice they bring to their deliberations. A generation has grown up since the last time this book was reprinted in this country, so thanks are due to Academy for this new edition.

Peter Shaffer, **Amadeus** (Signet, $3.50). A tremendous success, first as a play and later as a movie, **Amadeus** can still be read with enjoyment after one has seen it in either medium. For centuries there has been speculation whether Antonio Salieri, a journeyman composer, well positioned in Vienna's royal circles, had murdered Mozart. Don't expect a conventional murder plot or even a true resolution of the question, but instead enjoy "mystery" through a wonderful writer's insights into the nature of genius.

Ted Wood, **Live Bait** (Bantam, $2.95). Moonlighting as a security guard at a Toronto construction site while on vacation from his position as the one-man police force of Murphy's Harbour, Ontario, Reid Bennett proves he is just as adept in a big city as in the country. I find Bennett the best new series character to have come along in years, a mixture of brains, humanity, and physical skills. The author shows great taste and discipline in his balancing of these traits. Added interest is provided in the series by Reid's German Shepherd, Sam, and the policeman's intelligent references to the Viet Nam War in which he, though a Canadian, served. He wisely treats it as a war of individual honor, rather than one of political right or wrong. This is the third book in the Bennett series, and I heartily recommend it as well as its predecessors, both also available from Bantam: **Dead in the Water** and **Murder on Ice**.

THE MYSTERY OF MONBODDO

More than forty years ago, in the March 1945 issue of EQMM, Lillian de la Torre published a short story called "Dr. Sam: Johnson and Monboddo's Ape Boy." (It has recently been reprinted by International Polygonics as part of the de la Torre collection, **Dr. Sam: Johnson, Detector**, in trade paperback for $5.00. Though fiction, it is based on an actual visit Johnson and James Boswell made to Lord Monboddo's Scottish estate in 1773, while en route to the Hebrides.

Well known in the eighteenth century for his eccentric life style, Monboddo is best remembered today for his unsuccessful attempt to prove that some human beings retained tails, part of his belief that apes and man were related. When a famous ape at London's zoo died in 1960, the mystery writer Peter Dickinson wrote the following in **Punch**:

> Monboddo believed the orangoutan was human,
> Had a sense of ethics, was able to play the flute
> And differed from civilized man in his fine decorum
> And in being mute.

Writing of Monboddo's works in the areas of metaphysics and anthropology, a critic who was his contemporary called him "the owner of a most kindly heart, the author of most unreadable books."

(Continued on page 26.)

REEL MURDERS
MOVIE REVIEWS
by Walter Albert

In my last column I wrote about my 1984 Memorial Day weekend in Columbus, Ohio, where I attended—as I had for several previous years—the annual film festival sponsored by the Columbus Cinephiles. That Memorial Day custom is still one of the happiest events of the Spring for me and, to celebrate the revival of **The Mystery Fancier**, I should like to review some of the highlights of the 1985 and 1986 festivals.

Cinevent usually features films from the silent and early sound period and while the range is broad enough to satisfy the most eccentric of tastes, I shall only review films that suit the specialized tastes of the readers of this magazine.

It's in the Bag. United Artists, 1945. Director: Richard Wallace. Screen treatment: Lewis R. Foster, Fred Allen. Screenplay: Jay Dratler, Alma Reville. Alma Reville is, of course, Mrs. Alfred Hitchcock and I would like to think that some of the comic bite of this film reflects the deliciously wicked humor of the Hitchcock films. Many of the players in this crime comedy were better known for their work in radio than in films, and I must confess that some of my least happy hours as a child were spent watching the disappointing spectacle of radio material that did not work on the screen. This, I am delighted to report, is a happy exception to that experience, from the opening commentary by Fred Allen, as he "reads" the credits to the audience, to the satisfying conclusion. There is a gallery of funny supporting performances: William Bendix as a tender-hearted gangster leader who doesn't like violence (he inherited the mob from his mother); Jerry Colonna as a neurotic psychiatrist; Don Ameche, Victor More, and Rudy Vallee joining Allen to form one of the most improbable—and worst—barbershop quartets you are ever likely to hear; Dickie Tyler as Allen and Binne Barnes' precocious, unbearable son (with Allen's bags under his eyes); and the unflappable Robert Benchley, who delivers a comic monologue that is one of the two comedy highlights of the film (his son "invented" an aquarium that he converted into a universal mouse trap requiring some remarkable gymnastics from a gullible mouse; as Allen puts it: "Why would a mouse go to all that trouble to get a piece of cheeze instead of going into a restaurant like everybody else?"). The other highlight is also unrelated to the main plot (Allen has been left a fortune by an eccentric uncle who hid the money in one of the five chairs he also left his nephew) as Allen and his family enter a movie theater to see a zombie film for which they are promised immediate seating. It very quickly becomes clear that there are no seats available, and for about ten hilarious minutes the increasingly desperate group attempts to find seats. The film turns up occasionally on TV and I can recommend it for prime time or late night viewing.

The Gracie Allen Murder Case. Paramount, 1939. Director: Alfred E. Green. Script by Nat Perrin, based on a novel by S.S. Van Dine. The bomb of the convention and the opening sentence of the program note tells it all: "After distinguished portrayals by William Powell, Basil Rathbone, Paul Lukas, and Edmund Lowe, Philo Vance in the person of Warren William finally met his match in Gracie Allen." So did the film. Van Dine may have deserved this, but the competent cast (Jerome Cowan, Donald MacBride, H.B. Warner, and William Bendix) did not. After a scene in which the courtly, distinguished silent screen star H.B. Warner was abused by the abrasive and insensitive Allen in a bit of business that struck a new low in boorishness, I left the screening room. The actors were trying to ignore her; unfortunately, I could not.

Arsene Lupin. MGM, 1932. Director: Jack Conway. Adapted from the stage play by Maurice Leblanc and Francis de Croisset. John Barrymore plays Lupin and Lionel Barrymore is Inspector Guerchard, with Karen Morley playing a criminal who agrees to help Guerchard trap Lupin in exchange for her freedom. There is some disagreement among the various characters on the proper pronunciation of "Arsene," with Lionel the most skillful at mispronouncing it, but this is a charming film climaxed by a spectacular theft of the Mona Lisa from the Louvre. Morley, predictably, falls in love with Lupin; the Lupin character is laundered in the final scene to provide a conventional ending, and the transition from play to movie is not always successful. But John Barrymore plays the gentleman master criminal with an ease and casualness that give the film an illusion of freshness and spontaneity, while Morley is a beautiful and elegant foil to the two brothers.

The Unknown. MGM, 1927. Director: Tod Browning. One of Lon Chaney's most famous roles. He plays Alonzo, an armless circus performer, who loves Manon (Joan Crawford), daughter of the circus owner. Alonzo performs prodigious feats with his bare feet and is caressed fondly by Crawford, who cannot bear to be touched by "normal" men. Eventually, Crawford is cured of her neurosis and is happily married to the strongman, who has devised an act where his arms are attached to two horses running in place on treadmills with the mechanism controlled by a single lever in the wings. Alonzo, insane with jealousy, gains control of the lever and, as a horrified Crawford watches, speeds up the treadmill, the horses straining at their ropes, so that.... But you didn't think I was going to tell you how this one came out, did you? There's a strangulation murder, a dwarf, a visit to a hospital operating room at midnight (this is, after all, only four years before **Frankenstein**), and Chaney's menacing, brooding presence, like a tightly-wound spring that threatens to unwind at any time.

Michael Shayne, Private Detective. 20the Century Fox, 1940. Director: Eugene Forde. Screenplay by Stanley Rauh and Manning O'Conner based on a novel by Brett Halliday (no specific title was given). Lloyd Nolan plays Mike Shayne; Marjorie Weaver is the spirited female protagonist; Joan Valerie plays the femme fatale; Donald MacBride is the irascible, incompetent police chief with an even dumber but less irascible sidekick, Michael Morris; Walter Able, Douglas Dumbrille, Clarence Kolb, and George Meeker impersonate a quartet of heavies and candidates for chief murder suspect; and Irving Bacon, who was regularly flattened by Arthur Lake as he tried to deliver the mail to the Bumstead residence in the popular Columbia series, has a cameo as a fisherman neatly manipulated by Shayne into concealing testimony that would have implicated Shayne in the murder. This is a race-track, night-club mystery and is notable for two things: some really dumb situations for Shayne (his car stalls at the murder scene as the police are arriving; he throws what he believes to be the murder weapon--his own gun--into the bushes from which he handily retrieves it the next day after the police have presumably searched the area; he sticks his head into a dark room into which a man with a gun has just fled and is knocked out by the mug; and, in the hoariest and most predictably resolved plot gimmick in the film, he stages a mock murder using ketchup as blood and, when he attempts to play out his mini-drama, discovers that the ketchup has been enriched with some very real blood from a fatal bullet wound); and the introduction of a Little Old Lady detective (Elizabeth Patterson) whom he embraces at the end as his "partner" while he whispers to her, "And we'll split the money." I have not seen one of these Lloyd Nolan Shayne films in forty years. I would hope the others in the series have aged better. Patterson is a graceful actress who makes the best of an awkward role. She has read all the Ellery Queen mysteries and the Baffle Book and she keeps wanting to share a particularly difficult "baffle" with Shayne. Superior to **The Gracie Allen Murder Case**, but you may not see that as a recommendation.

Taxi. Warner Bros., 1932. Director: Roy del Ruth. Screenplay by "Gleason and Bright." James Cagney and Loretta Young, and a cameo by George Raft (as the winner of a dance contest; Cagney outsteps him all the way but the dance-hall audience registers its approval for the Raft team). Cagney and his brother (George E. Stone) are taxi drivers caught in a Manhattan taxi war. Young is the daughter of "Pops," a taxi-driver played by Guy Kibbee, murdered by the mob-run opposing taxi company. Cagney believes in fighting, not compromising, and when a truce is arranged he is outraged and convinced no good will come of it. When his brother is killed, Cagney goes on a one-man vendetta and it's a toss-up whether his brother's killer, the police, or his temper will get him first. William Everson characterizes this as a "tough, cocky comedy-melodrama." The comedy is supplied by Young's waitress friend, Marie, played by Dorothy Burgess. The character's whine gets a bit tiring after a while, but there is no gainsaying the skill with which Burgess plays this role. The movie is short (seventy minutes), and Cagney delivers his "you dirty yellow dog" line with an appropriate snarl. All the familiar Cagney mannerisms are used to good effect, and Young has a few moments in which she doesn't have that plastic look she adopted for most of her career. Minor Cagney and Warner Bros. melodrama but fun and has a very striking opening behind the credits with some jazzy editing setting the big city/taxi war context. The resolution is weak.

The Story of Temple Drake. Paramount, 1933. Director: Stephen Roberts. Screenplay by Oliver H.P. Garrett from William Faulkner's novel, **Sanctuary**. Cinematography by Karl Struss. According to the program notes (by William Everson), this, along with Warners' **Convention City**, finally precipitated the Production Code clean-up of 1934. Sordid but somewhat sanitized version of Faulkner's novel about a judge's daughter (Temple Drake, played by Miriam Hopkins) who is kidnapped, witnesses a murder, is raped, lives with the murderer for some time until she is driven to murder him, and finally "tells all" in a courtroom sequence wrapped up with lawyer/would-be boyfriend William Gargan's statement that he's "proud of her courage." Jack Larue (serial regular) is a slick, big-city villain ("Trigger"), ravisher of small-town hot stuff, Temple, who is used to promising more than she

(Continued on page 16.)

VERDICTS Book Reviews

Robert B. Parker. **Taming a Sea-horse.** Delacorte, 250 pp., $15.95.

Susan's back and Spenser's got her, which is good news for fans of Robert B. Parker's macho but sensitive private eye. The aberrations and depressions of the previous three books (**The Widening Gyre, Valediction,** and **A Catskill Eagle**) are wiped out and their consequences barely remarked. Life is back to normal in Spenser's thirteenth outing, which means rescuing damsels in distress—in this case one he already rescued in **Ceremony**.

April Kyle was a teenage runaway the wisecracking detective found hooking in Boston's Combat Zone. Since she was hooked on "the life," he placed her with a high-class Manhattan madam, Patricia Utley (from **Mortal Stakes**). In **Taming a Sea-horse**, April has left Utley's callgirl operation for an improbable pimp/Juilliard student named Rambeaux. (If this is a pun, he's not much like his namesake, being "almost fast enough to hit Spenser," and is soon dispatched.)

Spenser's quest is to find those responsible for killing him and Ginger Buckey, another prostitute, just to keep their identities secret. In looking for April Kyle, Spenser stirs up a number of wasps' nests, leading to the deaths of more-or-less innocent people. The theme is the big-business involvement of higher-ups (bankers and the Mob) in the sex industry, as it was in **Ceremony**. In fact, this is largely a rehash of the latter, which was a better book: Spencer finds April, Spenser loses April, Spenser finds April.... Nothing is resolved by the anticlimactic ending, leaving room for further chapters in the "saving" of April Kyle.

Taming a Sea-horse lacks most of the gratuitous violence for which Parker has been criticized. For instance, Spenser spraypaints the hair of a couple of hoods whom in earlier books he would have physically punished for several pages. Susan Silverman remarks (about his rescuing her in **Eagle**): "Whatever you did, and whoever you killed,... you were doing what you felt you had to do, and you were doing it for love." What he did for love was pointless and coldblooded murder. Susan goes on, "You ought not to forget that whoever you killed last year, there were people you could have killed and didn't." As Kathleen Turner said in **Prizzi's Honor**, "That's not very many, compared to the population as a whole."

There's a violent **High-Noon**-type confrontation with Ginger's sexually abusive father in which we are surely rooting for Spenser. Patricia Utley says, "Filing away Vern Buckey's name for future reference is perfect you. You feel compassion for her suffering and anger at his cruelty and competition in his toughness. You want to save her, punish him, and prove you're tougher. Man/boy.

Lover/killer. Savior/bully." Come on, Parker! People just don't talk like that, even high-class New York madams. (Meredith Phillips)

Marcia Muller. **The Cavalier in White.** St. Martin's, 207 pp., $15.95.

In spite of Susan's consciousness-raising lectures and Spenser's gourmet cooking, Parker's viewpoint is thoroughly masculine. (Note: for women readers unacquainted with the series, **Early Autumn** and **Looking for Rachel Wallace** are the most appealing introductions.) In contrast, a new breed of women detective writers is "redefining the genre by applying different sensibilities and values," as Marilyn Stasio wrote in the **New York Times Book Review.** They include Sara Paretsky, Julie Smith, Shelley Singer, Susan Dunlap, and three with new books: Marcia Muller, Mickey Friedman, and Sue Grafton. Paretsky's PI sleuth V.I. Warshawsky is the toughest; maybe being from Chicago she has to be. The others are Californians, and all except Grafton hail from the Bay Area.

Marcia Muller (besides co-editing numerous anthologies and reviewing mysteries in the **Chronicle**) has made her name with two different series featuring sleuths Sharon McCone and Elena Oliverez. **The Cavalier in White** is art security expert Joanna Stark's debut. Muller's strong points are interesting, under-used settings (the deYoung Museum, China Basin, Hunter's Point, Devil's Slide) and clever plotting. The book moves slowly but rewards the reader with constant uncovering of secrets and a surprise ending.

Muller's research on museum security (including insurance companies' standard methods of dealing with art thieves) is thorough but sometimes overwhelming. Stark lacks McCone's toughness and Oliverez's warmth, but she becomes more multi-faceted by the end, and future books will presumably flesh out the character. (Meredith Phillips)

Mickey Friedman. **Paper Phoenix.** E.P. Dutton, 183 pp., $15.95.

Like Joanna Stark, Mickey Friedman's Maggie Longstreet, the protagonist in **Paper Phoenix,** is a woman in her early forties, at first in retreat and semi-crippled by dependence on a man she's lost. Both have college-aged only children with whom they have to form new mature relationships. Absorption in a job, plus fending off danger (and affairs with new men), give them renewed self-assurance.

For a first novel (it was actually written before Friedman's two others; "phoenix" refers to the book, as well as Longstreet and San Francisco), **Paper Phoenix** is written with smooth authority, vivid characterization, and a unique voice. Friedman, former book editor of the **Examiner** now living in New York, has a good grasp of San Francisco sensibilities and people, and the book is leavened with witty, ironic observations: "... post-hippie style--much the same as hippie style, but without fringe and beads...." (Meredith Phillips)

Sue Grafton. **"C" is for Corpse.** Henry Holt, 243 pp., $14.95.

Sue Grafton's likable PI Kinsey Milhone is younger and tougher than Joanna Stark and Maggie Longstreet: a new generation, bang up to date. She not only runs, she pumps iron; she gets shot; she's unattached to family, home, or possessions; she's friendly with all sorts and ages of people. She's romantically vulnerable but never victimized, and she's sexually free.

In **"C" Is for Corpse** Milhone must investigate the death of a rich youth whom an earlier car accident had left crippled and amnesiac. An interesting subplot involves her landlord/friend with a predatory lady Milhone unmasks. Screenwriter Grafton conveys an excellent sense of place (a re-named Santa Barbara), and this successor to **"A" Is for Alibi** and **"B" Is for Burglar** leaves us eagerly awaiting **"D" Is for Deadbeat**. (Meredith Phillips)

Emma Page. **Every Second Thursday.** Walker, 196 pp., $2.95.

Detective-Chief Inspector Kelsey's restless habit of staring out any handy window precipitates the investigation in **Every Second Thursday;** his penchant for exchanging a word or two with any passing acquaintance provokes the culminating action. In between, Kelsey and Lambert, his Detective-Sergeant, engage in some splendid police work, none of which would have been undertaken, all of which will have come to naught, except for the lucky coincidences Emma Page describes so persuasively. This crafty combination of chance, logic, and careful detection is one appeal of this sound novel. Another is Page's ability to create diverting secondary characters.

It is not that Kelsey (who is dieting during this case and consequently thinking about food much of the time) and Lambert aren't interesting; they are. But they are also kept at some distance from the reader--we don't really get to know them well. The suspects in this inverted mystery are a man and woman defined by their coolness--each is aloof, controlled, and, of necessity, known to readers only through the detectives' speculations and through the comments of local folk the officers interrogate. The victim is rather better known to Page's audience; readers meet Vera Murdoch Foster in the early scenes, watch with her through part of the day of her death, and share Kelsey and Lambert's efforts to understand details of Vera's past and nuances of her personality as the policemen attempt to prove that Mrs. Foster did not commit suicide but was murdered. But Vera is not a very likable character: a daddy's darling conveniently married to a younger man, a perpetual girl who dreads the onset of age, Vera is very nearly stereotypical, is pitiful rather than sympathetic or interesting. Consequently, it's not really concern that Vera be avenged which propels the action but rather curiosity about how Vera's husband and her nurse could possibly have disguised murder as suicide so effectively. The major figures engage our intellects, not our emotions.

Not so the secondary characters. Vera's housekeeper, Alma Driscoll, is a feisty, pragmatic person with a good bit of family feeling--she keeps an eye on her aged uncle who is famous for staying just-this-side-of-the-law; maintains a brisk and apparently satisfying social life; handles her difficult employer and a collateral assignment (source of the title) with aplomb; and amuses readers into the bargain. Much more briefly but even more tellingly depicted is old Hetty Attwood, formerly housekeeper for the Murdochs and Fosters. Hetty's report of the Murdoch-Foster menage not only provides vital information but also allows for one of Page's masterly mini-portraits. It's superior. These women, along with Alma's uncle, the poacher-cadger Matt Bateman and several splendidly realized minor characters, give the book heart.

In **Every Second Thursday,** then, Page brings off her expected blend of intriguing situation, engaging characterization, and psychological substance. It's very satisfying. (Jane S. Bakerman)

Laurence Henderson. **Major Inquiry.** Academy Chicago, 1986, 192 pp., $4.95.

The back cover of Laurence Henderson's **Major Inquiry** announces that Academy. Chicago intends to publish more Detective Sergeant Milton adventures. If this novel is any measure, that's good news. Henderson's characters ring true; his setting strikes just the right balance between the placidly familiar and the newly horrific when murder invades a North London neighborhood; and the interactions of the large cast of characters are satisfyingly (and necessarily) intricate without slowing the tempo.

Indeed, pace is a major strength of this fine novel. When Monica Henekey, sixteen, is murdered, police immediately suspect a serial killer-rapist who has been attacking young working women for over a year. The massive search for him—and for anyone else who may be involved should there also be copycats at large—expands to include the Henekey case as well as the staff of the local precinct, and the consequent interactions of "locals" with "outsiders" forms a complex subplot whose intensity speeds the action along. Henderson conveys the quickened heartbeats of policewomen used as bait to catch the killer even as he depicts the painful slowness of the moments just before an expected attack. He shows the frenzied anxiety of the public (and the investigators) in contrast to the deliberate pace of the necessary checking, double-checking, and filing routines which must accompany more dramatic police work such as questioning witnesses or setting up entrapment teams. This technique is not unique to Henderson, but he handles it as well as anyone, better than most.

Excellent characterization is another of Henderson's many skills. Here, a broad range of characters is presented, usually by means of a brief description or with just a few lines of dialogue; yet each personality is clear and distinct. The central character, Detective Sergeant Arthur Milton, is deceptively nondescript. An older man who hasn't risen much in rank, a married man whose marriage has settled into dependable ordinariness, a good neighbor who can be counted on not to cause trouble and to lend a helping hand, he is also an individualist who employs a very effective combination of observation, instinct, and intuition in his work. Milton is a fascinating character, though he would be the last to think so.

Henderson is a good stylist who sometimes surprises. When one expects the end-of-the-chapter hook, Henderson very often substitutes a stop-em-in-their-tracks right cross, a startling but effective device which contributes heavily to the dark mood of this story. When Milton's wife, for instance, wonders what good the capture of the killer will do Mary's grieving mother, Milton replies, "None ... it never does." Later, a known offender rounded up for questioning complains about being a perpetual suspect: "'Every time something happens, the police come and say I did it. Every time a child is missing or gets hurt, every time, people look at me.' ... Potts [the suspect] walked out through the reception area. Everyone looked at him."

Potts' appearance is brief; he helps illustrate the attention to detail the police are focusing on this case; he contributes to the gritty realism which undergirds the story, and he does a bit more. When Henderson manages to create a sense of pity and horror in response to Potts, he's moving into territory usually reserved for mainstream rather than genre writers. The fact is, of course, as we crime fiction fans know, good writing is good writing wherever it appears, and half the fun of a formula comes from experimenting with it. Laurence Henderson experiments very successfully in **Major Inquiry**; in just about equal measure, he follows established police procedural formula and he surprises readers. He's very good. (Jane S. Bakerman)

Liza Cody. **Headcase**. Scribner's, 1986, 197 pp., $13.95.

Liza Cody began Anna Lee's adventures strongly in **Dupe** and followed with two other sound novels, **Bad Company** and **Stalker**; each time out, the characters have been a bit more vivid, Cody's hand a bit more sure. In **Headcase**, however, she's taken a giant step forward. In an unpublished interview, Cody said that she wouldn't want to continue the Anna Lee series if Anna ever stopped growing and changing. So far, so **very** good; **Headcase** shows plenty of growth for both author and protagonist.

As usual at Brierly Security, Mr. Brierly remains aloof, cold, demanding, and Beryl, his right-hand woman, continues to fight the operatives to a draw over every minute on the job, every farthing on the expense account. Currently, Beryl is introducing beepers so that the staff can be ever more handily at her beck and call. That's one subplot: the doings at the office, the fate of the beepers. The doings at home are another subplot: Selwyn and Bea, Anna's downstairs neighbors and extended family, give an amazing, impromptu party, and Selwyn, under the weather even more than usual, tries his hand at detecting (he doesn't like it) and at providing a substitute sleuth (he does pretty well at that). These complications give heft and dimension to Anna's life and thus expand her character. They also provide plenty of opportunity for humor, and it seems to me that in **Headcase** Cody takes better advantage of those opportunities than ever before.

Amid the fun, though, there are deadly games in progress, and on one level **Headcase** indicts people who use others as toys or pawns as fiercely as does any book by Parker, Paretsky, or Macdonald. Like Macdonald, Cody also excoriates adults who remain too immature to be effective parents. But despite the fact that the common concerns of hard-boiled private eye novels abound in **Headcase** (as in Cody's earlier works), Anna Lee and her assignments are clearly and specially Cody's own. Cody knows the PI territory and is busy carving out her own portion of it.

Asked by Mr. and Mrs. Rodney Hahn to trace their teenaged daughter, Thea, Anna discovers that the girl follows an astoundingly orderly, controlled, disciplined routine. The fact that Thea is a genius doesn't account, Anna feels, for the total absence of frivolity or even liveliness in the girl's life. As she discovers that Thea has conducted another, secret life which has shattered her personality and put her at odds with the law, Anna also uncovers the clandestine activities of several adults. Some characters in **Headcase** pretend to great virtue, but once again Anna Lee and her fans discover that people who admit their faults are less dangerous to others, are particularly less dangerous to the innocent young. Anna does what she can for Thea, a memorable character; she supports another likable teenager, Sam Tulloch, and she is herself supported by one of Selwyn's better finds, the gigantic, always hungry Quex, who has the soul of a poet, a heart of gold--and a job on an oil rig. That job is a great convenience; it could allow Cody to send him off to the

North Sea or bring him back at will, and I like Quex enough that I hope he appears again.

These folks, along with the other good guys in the cast of continuing characters—Bea, Selwyn, Bernie, and Syl—help to offset the ineffectual parents, the selfish housewives, the sniveling peeper, and the grasping hotel employees among whom Anna moves as she tries to protect Thea from a murder charge. Cody strikes a fine balance between the wonderfully ridiculous, the painfully ordinary, the coldly selfish, and the downright deadly—it all adds up to a strong, realistic novel. **Headcase** is a must read. (Jane S. Bakerman)

Lawrence Block. **When the Sacred Ginmill Closes.** Arbor House, 1986, 239 pp., $16.95.

It's boom time in the private eye business, or more precisely in the private eye **writing** business. So many PI novels are coming at us nowadays that not even speed readers can keep up. but with all the prosperity for authors and publishers in the field, with all the academic dissertations on the eye as American mythic hero, at times we miss the simplicity with which PI fiction began, we think back nostalgically to when the eye wasn't carrying the dead weight of cultural significance on his trenchcoated shoulders. Those are the times for rereading Dashiell Hammett—or for curling up with the latest PI novel of Lawrence Block.

Like Hammett, Block writes a clean and simple line, uncluttered by the profusion of metaphors and similes we associate with Raymond Chandler and Ross Macdonald. Block's eye, Matt Scudder, doesn't ruminate morosely on the human condition and the state of his own soul, in the manner of all too many contemporary private eyes. Indeed he's not even a licensed professional like hammett's characters. Scudder is a former New York cop who, after accidentally killing a Puerto Rican child in a street gunbattle, turned in his badge and reached for the bottle. As of 1975, the time of **When the Sacred Ginmill Closes**, his life is a lurch from bar to bar, his only friends a small group of convivial drunks like himself, his only source of income the money he gets for doing investigative or body-guarding work under the counter for boozing acquaintances. In this sixth book-length adventure, Scudder drifts into three criminal situations—the stickup of an after-hours joint with ties to the IRA, the murder of a Brooklyn woman whose philandering husband is prime suspect, and the theft of secret account books from one of Scudder's regular bars—and the three eventually merge into two, but whether the two ever merge into one you'll have to read the book to find out.

If you're looking for fast pace, violent action, and convoluted plotting, please look somewhere else. Block has structured this novel in the rhythm of his protagonist's life: aimless, meandering, purposeful only at odd moments. The author is at his best evoking offbeat corners of Manhattan and Brooklyn and describing the crazy quirky conversations of Scudder and his saloon compadres, which almost make this sad and sodden lifestyle seem worthwhile. Plot connoisseurs won't be happy with the book's climax, nor will devotees of conventional morality. Even the morally unconventional may wonder why Scudder's brand of private justice against a legally unreachable bad guy is okay while his friend Skip's very similar brand of private justice is treated as dubious. But it's amazing how purely readable a pro like Block can make a PI novel without help from the elements that fuel most books of this type. **When the Sacred Ginmill**

Closes is a bit of an oddball, but just right for the PI fan who wants for a few hours to take a detour from the well travelled main roads of the genre. (Francis M. Nevins, Jr.)

Georges Simenon. **Justice.** Harcourt Brace Jovanovich, 1985, 176 pp., $13.95.

Emotionally devastated by tragedies described in his autobiography and in books about him by others, Simenon gave up writing fiction fifteen years ago and now lives in retirement in a simple Swiss villa near Lausanne. But he was so miraculously prolific between the late twenties and the early seventies that his American publishers are still putting out several titles a year which are new in the United States, about evenly divided among mainstream novels, non-series crime novels, and the cases of European literature's greatest detective, Maigret.

Justice falls into the second of these categories, was written in August of 1937, published in France in 1941 as **Cour d'assises** (which is the name of the French court where the most serious criminal cases are tried), and released in England in 1949. Why another thirty-six years went by before it came out over here is beyond comprehension, for it's one of the finest psychological suspense novels he ever wrote. With the vivid sensuous detail that is his trademark, Simenon evokes the last free days in the life of Petit Louis, a happy-go-lucky minor thief and gigolo. Just when his financial and sexual affairs are smoothly humming along, he's framed by treacherous underworld pals for the murder of the wealthy middle-aged woman he'd been living with and systematically stealing from. He goes on the run, gets caught, and is put on trial by an absurd criminal justice system which hates him less for his legal offenses than for the fact that he's an unrepentant nonconformist and outsider.

If this brief description sounds just a bit familiar, it's probably because the story line is more than a little like that of perhaps the most famous French novel of this century, Albert Camus' **The Stranger.** It's not clear whether the similarities are coincidental. The Camus classic was published in France in 1942, only a year after **Cour d'assises,** which isn't much of a time lapse and therefore suggests coincidence. On the other hand, both novels were published by the same French house, Gallimard, and it's possible that Camus could have seen or known of the Simenon before it came out. There are enough similarities in detail--the vivid sun-soaked atmosphere, the emphasis in the trial scenes on the defendant's cold relationship with his mother, the contemptuous spurning of the prison chaplain near the climax--so that anyone who's read both novels can't help but suspect a strong Simenon influence on Camus.

The final verdict on that issue I leave to the scholars. On the book itself I pass my own judgment. If you want a model of European crime fiction, full of strong characterizations and cinematic evocations of setting, combining suspense and a sense of inevitability, you can't go wrong with this Simenon. (Francis M. Nevins, Jr.)

John Lutz. **The Right to Sing the Blues.** St. Martin's, 1986, 175 pp. $14.95.

The up-to-date private eye is closer to Alan Alda than to Bogart and hangs out almost anywhere but California. Contemporary

PI writers want to forge the same symbiotic relationship between The Eye and The City that Spade had with San Francisco and Marlowe with LA, but the cities they choose tend to be in the midwest. Loren Estleman uses Detroit, Jonathan Valin opts for Cincinnati, Michael Lewin picks Indianapolis, and the St. Louis area's foremost mystery novelist has, understandably enough, set his private eye series in and around St. Louis.

Our local PI is named Alo Nudger—although that awful first name is mentioned almost never—and works out of an office above a Danny's Donuts emporium in a seedy suburb of St. Louis County. What sets him apart from other eyes? For one thing, unlike 99% of his fictional colleagues, he does not narrate his cases in first person. More important, he comes close to being a total loser, plagued by overdue bills and a greedy ex-wife and ripoff consumer goods and a nervous stomach requiring roll after roll of antacid tablets and most of all by his own near-paralyzing unaggressiveness and compassion. A movie director who wanted to catch the essence of this character wouldn't cast Alan Alda (too macho) but would hunt for someone like the Chaplin of **City Lights**. To make such a protagonist work plausibly in PI fiction has to be a hair-greying challenge, but John Lutz is more than equal to it, and Nudger has appeared in several magazine stories plus three novels, of which the best, and the most saturated with the St. Louis scene, is **Nightlines** (1984).

The Right to Sing the Blues has a few chapters set in St. Louis but unfolds mainly in New Orleans. A French Quarter jazz club owner has hired Nudger to find out what's behind the relationship between the world-class jazz pianist who is his primo attraction and a Bourbon Street blues singer who happens to be the daughter of the local crime czar. The resulting round of murders, beatings, betrayals, threats and emotion traps forces Nudger to keep well stocked with antacid tablets until all the pieces of the puzzle start to make sense. Those who think as I do that **Nightlines** was one of the decade's finest PI novels will definitely want to catch Lutz's latest number, a strong satisfying book in which the **noir** overtones of character and plot are counterpointed by the sounds of what he calls "the music of the lost." (Francis M. Nevins, Jr.)

John Lutz. **The Right to Sing the Blues**. St. Martin's, 1986, $14.95.

Private eye Al Nudger is a typical PI--divorced, out of money, ex-cop, mid-forties, now involved with a good, wholesome woman. At one point he turns down $20,000 rather than walk away from the investigation he was hired to carry out. After all, this man has "Ethics," as he tells the luscious, leather-panted lady who tries to bribe him. He also gets beaten by experts, leaving no bruises or broken bones, only a little blood in his urine. But that doesn't bother Nudger. He has enough experience in these things to know he'll stop bleeding in a few days. No need to see a doctor.

All this activity (as well as the murder of an old jazz/blues star) is the result of Nudger's job of looking into the background of an excellent but off-key piano player. Hollister, the "keyboard sensation," has gotten rather deeply involved with Ineida Collins, a second-rate singer who happens to be the daughter of a local underworld boss. Protection for Ineida is the underlying motivation of much of the novel.

Lutz has a slightly sardonic attitude toward his characters. Nudger knows he is following the pattern of thousands of private eyes who have gone before him. He is able to remain detached (or resigned) as he goes through the rituals of explaining his moral code, and getting worked over. The average characterization does not detract from the agreeableness and pleasure of the story. Lutz knows his PI conventions and does a fine job of maneuvering the pieces. (Fred Dueren)

John D. MacDonald. **The Lonely Silver Rain.** Knopf, 1985. (**WARNING: Numerous plot developments revealed herein.**)

The latest Travis McGee novel to date and number twenty-one in the series is dedicated to Mystery Fanciers Jean and Walter Shine. The dedication is a quality gesture on MacDonald's part proving some of the nice things Jean and Walter say about him are true.
Billy Ingraham, one of Travis McGee's buddies from the house-boating set, outfits and provisions the **Sundowner**, a custom cruiser built in the Jacksonville yard and worth seven-hundred-and-twenty-thousand dollars, and takes it on a test run in preparation for a honeymoon trip up the Waterway to New England with his new bride Millis. Billy and Millis are on a sandbar island hunting for little purple shells so she can string a necklace, he in his trunks and Millis as "naked as an egg," when someone boards the **Sundowner** and drives it away, right before their eyes, and they are left in the condition described above with a hundred-and-ninety dollar Danforth anchor and ten feet of rubber-coated anchor chain.
Ingraham strikes a deal with Travis McGee to hunt for the **Sundowner**. By application of a helpful hint from Meyer, his hairy economist friend and fellow houseboat owner, McGee finds the stolen boat in a few days. It has three dead people aboard, no live ones. Two of the bodies are of the young man and woman who had apparently stolen it, and the third is the daughter of a Peruvian diplomat. The **Sundowner** is in such sad shape that Billy Ingraham spends eighty-eight thousand to get it cleaned up and the smell out of it. He has lost all desire to honeymoon with Millis on it.
Then Billy Ingraham dies with a massive cerebral hemorrhage in a hotel in Cannes, France, a hemorrhage which turns out to have been induced by something like a length of piano wire sharpened at one end and stuck into the inside corner of his left eye. And McGee gets a small package the size of a book which blows up the two boys who steal it from his car. Who killed Billy Ingraham and wants Travis McGee dead and why? Of course, as you would expect, McGee does his sex-duty performance with Ingraham's spicy young widow, Millis, and thereby saves her health, mind, and life. I have never been an undoubting believer in the medicinal powers of Travis McGee's sex organs, and now, after what seems like the thousandth despairing woman he has bedded and healed, his bed 'em and save 'em routing has begun to come across like a trick of charlatan quackery.
The Lonely Silver Rain is a book that I will reread. MacDonald uses a more restrained style and takes more care with his writing than usual, that is, to a point beyond half-way in the book. But from there MacDonald goes off on a tangent, the plot fizzles, the ending is tacked on, and the story MacDonald started to tell is never quite finished. (Frank Floyd)

Harold Q. Masur. **Send Another Hearse.** A Raven House Mystery from Worldwide Library, 1980.

Does the first sentence or paragraph of a book every year or three really put the whammy on you? The following is the latest one for me: "She was vogue on the outside and vague on the inside." It is the opening sentence of **Send Another Hearse**. I read it and stopped. I knew that woman, knew how she was dressed, how she was made-up, and the part of society she belonged to, even her approximate age. Her mental state, too, but not what had caused it. How can any book live up the the expectation and hope with which a starting out like the line quoted above fills the breast?

Scott Jordan, Masur's Brooklyn-based series attorney, has been consulted by Adam Coleman, one half of Coleman & Varney, Literary Agents, because the Varney half has disappeared with two hundred thousand dollars paid the firm by Zenith Films for the rights to **The Kingpins**, a first book by a soured ex-cop, a thinly veiled account of the murder of a mob informant while in protective custody and the cover-up of police involvement. Eventually someone shoots Jordan's secretary as she looks out a peep-hole in his apartment door to see who is there. The killing off of this good and reliable old secretary was a flimsy effort to stir the plot, and I am still smarting over the unnecessary loss. Poor Cassidy was likable and useful and deserving of a kinder fate.

This is not the best Harold Q. Masur, but it is better than some writers' best. It is written well but not always wisely, and wisely but not always well.

As proof of my point, I offer a clear illustration from the author's own pen. Turn to page 117. "I saw his point and broke in impulsively. 'Of course. Whoever killed Duncan let the air out of that tire to make sure Adam couldn't drive away. Insurance that he'd be caught. We can prove that by showing there isn't any leak.'" This statement has more leaks than a house full of bad faucets. The flat tire which the speaker desires to show has no leaks has been driven on for some ways. The speaker is not some dumbcluck lawyer like the ones my friends hire--their lawyers are not that dumb--making this statement; this is the fictional whiz of our whodunit story speaking, trying to reassure his client who has been found driving around town on the flat tire in question with a dead body sitting in the car seat beside him. Unfortunately, someone deflates Scott Jordan, the whiz, by telling him that driving on a flat tire cuts it to ribbons. (Even his brilliant legal mind can discover no way of proving there is no leak in the flat tire after being told this.) Fortunately, the confidence Jordan's client has in him never wavers.

I am not anxiously waiting the next Scott Jordan outing, but I am waiting for it. (Frank Floyd)

Philip MacDonald. **Warrant for X**. Doubleday, Doran, 1938; Avon, 1973.

The opening chapter of **Warrant for X** has no peer for the slow, sure, smooth building of suspense. It introduces a book in which suspense continues to build, touched with humor to make the suspense bearable. It begins with a seemingly trivial incident in the life of Sheldon Garrett, an American playwright whose play has just opened successfully in London. Someone tells him about Chesterton's **Napoleon of Notting Hill** and he sits up all night reading it. The next day, a Sunday--and that's important to the plot--Garrett goes out to see Notting Hill for himself. Naturally he gets lost, wears his feet out, and stops in the first teashop he can find. There he overhears a conversation, the crucial conversation from which the whole book builds. The mood goes from discouragement to hope, from hope to excitement, from excitement to discouragement again. Then danger sets in, and thence, in the long, long run, come the unmasking and capture of some bold and wicked criminals.

The crucial conversation is between two women whose faces Garrett never sees. He can hear much of what they say, and when they leave he sees their backs. One is considering a proposal to be part of some undertaking which sounds illegal, for which she will be well paid. The other is by turns persuasive and threatening. There is a man named Evans somewhere, of whom the first woman is afraid. At last she agrees to whatever the proposal is; Garrett gathers that it involves the kidnapping of a child. There is also the possibility that a man will be killed. He trails the women to the underground when they leave, but then he loses them. On going back to the teashop to pay his bill, he finds that one of the women has left a glove behind. In it are a bus ticket and a shopping list. These are the only tangible clues.

The people he asks what they would do if they overheard a crime being planned don't take him seriously. Neither does Scotland Yard. In desperation he tells Avis Bellingham, the woman he loves. She understands, for she knows that his sister's child was kidnapped, and, though returned physically unharmed, was emotionally damaged. From this stems his horror of kidnapping, more immediate than that of the average person. It is Avis who introduces Garrett to Anthony Gethryn, wealthy amateur of crime, newspaper writer, and friend of officials at Scotland Yard. There could be no one better qualified to help track down the vanished plotters.

From the bus ticket Gethryn locates a neighborhood; from a scribble on the shopping list he deciphers a name and address hastily written. These lead to the first success; one of the women is Janet Murch, a nursemaid. But Murch is elusive. She has left her titled employer, and her only relative, an aunt, has gone to Scotland. The search widens; the employment agency she had used proves to be doing a thriving business in blackmail. This brings Scotland Yard into the picture.

Then Garrett is attacked, Avis's apartment is burgled, her maid struck down, and Avis herself disappears. Each turn of the suspense screw brings the reader closer to the edge of the chair, with quickened breathing. At long last Murch is traced to one or the other of two families who traveled to England from the United States on one ocean liner. Each is rich; each has a child; each child has a nursemaid. Again Gethryn and Garrett, with the aid of Lucas of Scotland Yard, are on the heels of the suspects. But one more red herring must be drawn across the trail before we all come to the conclusion, and the capture, at the last possible moment, of a pair of criminals.

There is always something happening, never a dull moment! There is fine detection, as minimal physical clues are followed to the identification and locating of human beings. Following a long trail was Philip MacDonald's strong suit; here, as in **The List of Adrian Messenger**, he provided rich detail, absorbing suspense, delightful humor, and a touch of love interest to leaven the mix, and came out with a story that still held this reader's interest right to the last page. (Maryell Cleary)

The Documents In the Case (Letters)

From Jeff Banks, P.O. Box 13007, SFA Sta., Nacogdoches, TX 75961:

The pleasure with which I welcome **The Mystery Fancier** back truly knows no bounds. In one of his earliest books, Ted Mark (Ted Gottfried) had one of his characters—actually she was an editorial worker on a magazine—struggling to find words to express "the liquid sounds of love"; my problem is similar. How does one put into words a pleasure that verges on the orgasmic? Perhaps you'll want to wear gloves to finish reading this letter? Anyway, I am DELIGHTED! And I'm sure many other of your readers feel the same!...

Here's a little curiosity I ran across while scanning a Texas Gazetteer for a Sesquicentennial project (which, characteristically, I never quite got around to finishing). I happened to notice there was a Chandler town name, and that set me to wondering how many other major mystery writers I could find immortalized on the Texas map. I came up with Hamilton, O'Donnel, Post, and Whitney, and I am sure I must have missed some others. But I was pleased that my state might seem to be immortalizing the creators of Phillip Marlowe, Matt Helm, Modesty Blaise, Randolph Mason and Uncle Abner, and perhaps the best of the romantic suspense novels.

That got me to looking for characters; I also noticed there is a Parker County (for the creator of Spenser, of course). Character names I found included Archer County, Mason County, Hunter, Malone, Mason, Trent, and West.

And that got me to looking at the gazetteers for the other states. (At this point some of your readers are concluding that I am rather underemployed to be spending my time this way.) Predictably for one who is proud to be a Texan, I found no other state coming close to Texas in seeming to commemorate the great heroes and writers of "our kind" of fiction. Also, I noticed that some of the names appeared much more frequently than others, and some of the greatest were completely (or almost so) neglected. I could find nothing else honoring Melville Davisson Post, and only Indiana seems to have a Poe. There were no Doyles or Christies. The names that showed up most frequently included Parker, 11 times; Gardner, 11; and Hamilton, 26. The moral to all this seems to be that if you happen to share a name with one of the Founding Fathers you are more likely to be a writer that is "on the map."

Perhaps the residents of other states may want to check my counting. Grab your gazetteers, folks.

Now, on to other matters.

I believe that my series of Spy Charts has pretty much run its course. Though I may update the Hamilton (there he is again) later.

I certainly hope that your letters column will be its old lively self in the revivified magazine. Only a few of the letters you used to publish were of the sort that I detest and find in most fan publications, no matter to which genre they may be devoted.

I also hope that you will share with your readers your career plans now that your legal studies are done. Do you plan to emulate Perry Mason (I hope not Randolph Mason, even though I love the stories about him)? How about John J. Malone? Actually, I guess you probably aren't planning to practice criminal law (wonderful phrase) at all, but I hope you will tell us!

What is upcoming from Brownstone Books? Here is an unsolicited testimonial: I feel that the books I bought, all but one, I believe, that you have published thus far, are tremendous bargains. I would have gladly paid more than the price asked for each and every one. (But I hope you aren't planning to bill me for more money for any of them now!)

Another concern of mine for your rebeginning period is cover art. I know that was one of the more difficult solicitations for you all through the original run of TMF (see what a good boy I'm being for the moment and not even calling the magazine "MFer" anymore!) and I imagine it could pose an even larger problem as you are getting started up again. One suggestion I have is that you might follow the lead of EQMM of a few years ago and use photographs on the covers. Instead of the great figures of Mystery Writing, I suggest your cover be graced for a few issues with photos of the top folk in Mystery Fandom--editors of the magazines, elected officials of the APA, folk in charge of recent and upcoming Bouchercons, and so on. You should begin with a cover depicting yourself; this need not be a pin-up or "beefcake" shot, nor would you need to be costumed as Sherlock, the Shadow, or Whoever--a portrait would do fine.

If you don't approve of the idea, I suppose you could give us an issue or two with stick figures on the cover ostensibly honoring the Saint while you pray for someone who can draw to come to your aid. I believe if you put the idea to your readers via the letter column, you will find much support for it. Also, if you reject the photo idea out of hand but **are** having difficulties getting cover art, I have at least one less conventional idea that I will share with you and your readers later.

From Maryell Cleary, 08627 Lake Shore Dr., Grand Junction, MI 49056:

Your plea for copy for issues of TMF to come was received, noted, and became a spur to action. Sad to say, my last few months have been hectic ones, so I never got as far as actually sending you anything. These are some retrospective reviews of mysteries in the pre-1940 or WWII days. I just got around to rewriting the drafts I did earlier on. I would be glad to have this be a regular feature--no more than one or two an issue, though, please! I think I could handle that small a number even during the work year. Maybe you could come up with a catchy title. I'm not very good at that. Of course you may want to print them in some other way, or not at all, and it's entirely up to you, natch.

I have been working intermittently on an article on the contemporary clerical detectives. The slant is quite different from the one taken in the recent TAD article. It's a big undertaking, even if the outcome may not be major in size. There's been a lot of reading, mostly good, and I've taken lots of notes. I've had a nice letter from Barbara Byfield re her Anglican priest-detective. I hope that this summer I can pull it all together.

TAD accepted my article on the books of Leslie Ford, but still has not printed it. Wish I'd left it with you! Ah, well, the things we don't know ahead of time.

From Fred Isaac, 1501 Milvia St., Berkeley, CA 94709:

I hasten to answer your note, for a variety of reasons. One is, of course, to congratulate you for finishing the grind and getting back to TMF again. There has been a significant gap in the field without you, which is probably why all of us stayed with it.

I figure you have been following Bob Napier's MDM for the past year. For my money it has been a good contact with the "real fan" community. I have been more than a little interested to note that there has been so much from the authors, and so little from anybody on the academic side. Hmmmm. This is what I was talking about in "Bleeding the Fun Out" three years ago. It makes very little sense, really. Anyway, MDM has been interesting, and does fill a gap. There seems not to have been many free-wheeling letters in the bigger magazines, and Dapa-Em has such a small group that the rest of us have been shut out.

From Frank Floyd, Rt. 3, Box 125-H, Berryville, AR 72616:

I've been thinking ... what I like to read about in other Mystery Fanciers' letters. I thought I would jot down a list so that Mystery Fanciers might decide to discuss some of these things when they write:

1. Writers or books they like or don't like. The interesting part is why they like or don't like them.
2. Out of the way or personal knowledge of mystery writers, not necessarily known ones, and of their books--including personal experiences.
3. Events related to the mystery field in which they have participated or to which they have gone.
4. What place reading mysteries fits into in their lives. What function it serves. What is its niche among the rest of the things they do.
5. Do they write or plan to do so?
6. Anything in their country or region of the country of general interest to Mystery Fanciers.
7. Their speculation on mystery topics, things that outrage them or that they think are villainous and definitely wrong, or things they think are definitely right, or ideas that they have which they think would improve something.
8. New developments in the field and new or old things that have failed or succeeded.
9. Personal experiences with other Mystery Fanciers.
10. Their opinion of the comparative merit of mystery and other types of literature.

I stop here not because this is everything but because it is probably enough, at least for now....

Having just finished reading **Murder in E Minor**, I have finally found use for the word aghast. That is what I am. Aghasted! I will report later when I have had an opportunity to become more unaghasted.

www.ingramcontent.com/pod-product-compliance
Lightning Source LLC
Chambersburg PA
CBHW031435040426
42444CB00006B/823